TEN HOUNDS:
A PERSONAL JOURNAL

*A Subjective Look at the Evolution of
Loyola University Maryland Men's Lacrosse*

by

G. Darrell Russell, Jr.

DORRANCE
PUBLISHING CO
EST. 1920
PITTSBURGH, PENNSYLVANIA 15238

Dorrance Publishing Co
585 Alpha Drive
Pittsburgh, PA 15238
Visit our website at dorrancebookstore.com

ISBN: 978-1-6480-4088-7
eISBN: 978-1-6480-4900-2

This is a sports tale based on faith, hope, and love

For all who have donned the Greyhound lacrosse helmet

Previous books by the author:
Lincoln and Kennedy: Looked at Kindly Together
Hotbed for Hybrids: Soccer and Lacrosse in Baltimore
Commoner to Royalty: A Judicial Journal

All drawings are by Martin "Skip" Barry, All American goalie from Loyola, 1950. They are reprinted with permission from his children, Martin Barry, Jr and Barbara Barry. The drawings were supplemented by sketches by Barbara Barry. Much thanks to the Barry family.

Thanks also to my paralegal, Nicole Warner, who is a wizard at Word Perfect, whereas your author is not.

CONTENTS

PRAYER OF SAINT IGNATIUS LOYOLA

Dear Lord,
Teach me to be generous,
Teach me to serve you as you deserve,
To give and not to count the cost,
To fight and not to heed the wounds,
To toil and not to seek for rest,
To labor and not to ask for any reward,
Save that of knowing that I do your will, O God.

"Lacrosse unbends the mind better than any other sport, because of the ubiquity of the ball; it is more genuine recreation, and is a holiday to the blood to play, and a half holiday to look on."

Dr. William George Beers

CHAPTER ONE:

LACROSSE BEGINS IN AMERICA

The game of lacrosse began with the American Indians. Consequently, it is often glorified as *the* true American game. More accurately, lacrosse is the true American game of the northeast of the USA and the southeast of Canada. Other sports did originate in America, notably the big three of football, basketball, and baseball. But those sports were started by non-Indian immigrants. Football was a bastardization of rugby, a European sport. European football became known as soccer in America. Basketball did begin with peach baskets on poles in New England by Dr. Naismith and non-Indian Puritans who claimed kinship to the Mayflower and Plymouth Rock adventures. Abner Doubleday began baseball in upper-state New York, allegedly in Cooperstown, where baseball is memorialized in the Hall of Fame. Ice hockey trickled down from Canada, which imported the game from the icy Scandinavian countries.

The Indians were the *true* early Americans who created lacrosse, as a "gift from the creator." They of course did not call themselves

Americans. Rather, they were identified by tribes, namely, Hurons, Cherokees, Creek, Mohicans, Sioux, Iroquois, or members of the six nation tribes. And this was their identity. And it was the Iroquois who, more than any other tribe, passed the game on to the white man. The Indians eventually were helpless as non-native enthusiasts restructured their game and imposed control over it. Between World Wars I and II, Americans gave modern structure to the game that is known as field lacrosse in the USA. At the same time, Canadians embraced box lacrosse, as it's known and played today.

Arguably, the creation of modern lacrosse occurred in Canada in 1867 when they adopted the game the Mohawks called Tewaaraton. The Ojibwe, from the Great Lakes region, called the game baggata-way. The Mohawks were part of the Iroquois' Confederacy. The Canadian parliament this year supposedly passed a series of rules and practices, which became a defining moment in giving structure to a raucous game. It all had begun when the Indians, in preparing for tribal wars and then later colonial wars, created this wild game that featured romps with sticks in hand over hill and dale. The Indians had many names for lacrosse, most eminent of which was baggata-way. Predecessors of today's Jesuit troubadours, who still educate, counsel, heal, build and govern, first traveled the American continent and observed the Indians' high-spirited game of baggataway. The Jesuits saw the curved sticks and were reminded of the French settlers' word for the bishop's crosier, *la-crosse*. The primitive game played by the Indians became known as *La Jeu de la Crosse*.

Historians believe the game was at one time played extensively across the continent. There is some proof of this assertion in the reality that many American cities throughout the USA are named Lacrosse. But with the white man's colonization, lacrosse vanished like the Indian's land, and the game remained only on both sides of the St. Lawrence River. That is, upper-state New York, New England,

4

Ontario and Quebec. The Indian's game flowed with the landscape. Goals ranged from village to village, often with several hundred braves to a side. But the numbers dwindled as the pace quickened. Fractures and fatalities were considered the breaks of the game. Boundaries were sketchy, so slashing behind the tee pees or mayhem behind the barn was rampant. It was considered honorable for a young warrior to perish during a game.

There were many other stark differences from the game played today beyond the number of players, the primitive sticks, and the lack of boundaries. The crude sticks were made of animal skin and tree branches. The Indians preferred running the ball rather than passing and did not employ the Hopkins Weave. The Indians played the game 90 percent naked, but the modern lacrosse player is outfitted in a plastic helmet, face mask, cleats, padded gloves, shoulder and arm pads, and to complete the ensemble, a pair of elongated shorts. The latter makes the player look like he started dressing and changed his mind. The Indians played the game not simply for recreation, but for religious, spiritual, and medicinal reasons. They called it, "the little brother of war." The game was extremely violent, so as to prepare young braves for close combat. The game was organized mayhem. But the Braves played with honor and dignity and in time significantly refined their game. This was prior to the action of a Dr. Walter Beers, who authored the Canadian Parliament Resolution of 1867, which supposedly proclaimed lacrosse as the nation's official sport, as well as passing some rules for the game. Years later, an examination of the minutes of Parliament showed that the measure was never formally voted on. But the supposition endures.

The Indians never condoned the blatant offense of hitting from behind. If a Brave played unfairly, he would remove himself from the game. Or the dirty play caused the squaws to run onto the field and beat the perpetrator. It is a popular misconception that even in today's game, dirty players notoriously gravitate to lacrosse because in the game, they can slake their devilish thirsts. It is indeed a riotous sport. Sticks and bodies do fly. The seeming alternative for the player is to skewer or be skewered. But refinement has come steadily to lacrosse. It has progressed to the point where it can be called a beautiful game. It is no longer an Indian substitute for war. And there have been no recorded fatalities of late.

L

On June 4, 1763, at a time of fragile peace between the Indians and settlers, the former invited the latter to an exhibition lacrosse game at Fort Michilimackinac, Michigan. After playing for a while, the Indians called time out and proceeded to turn their attention to the audience of settlers. With a sudden loss of peaceful feelings, they ruthlessly slaughtered the settlers. The Indians employed arrows and tomahawks in deference to lacrosse sticks. Then they retrieved their sticks and returned to the game. This obvious ruse of a game, a shocking historical fact, is the first recording of an actual contest. This game facilitated the overthrow of the British fort. However, in a matter of a few weeks, the British re-captured their fort.

I had a fun experience in playing for the University Club Collegians at Mackinac Island, Michigan in 1963. We earned this trip by virtue of winning the US Open title. We played three exhibition games against local Michigan teams in commemoration of the massacre two hundred years earlier at the nearby Fort Michilimackinac. The fort is gone now, of course, and so are the Indians. More exciting than the games, which we won handily, was a wonderful horse-drawn carriage ride around the wooded island, where cars are still not allowed. Hy Levasseur, All American midfielder from UVA and Boys Latin and his striking wife, Jocelyn, and I shared the buggy. The carriage driver was respectfully taciturn, and he let us visually absorb the historic island's summer villas without uttering verbal inanities. The horse had nothing to say either. The governor of Michigan has an official house on the island which is his summer residence. He didn't bother us either.

Almost a century later, historians recorded a second game. The American Revolution was over, with a win for America. Then the hostilities erupted again with Great Britain in the War of 1812, with another win for the USA. But no one recorded any lacrosse activity until 1834. The Indians played an inter-tribal scrimmage in Montreal, which was reported quite favorably in the weekly *Montreal Gazette*. Sportsmen of Montreal, infused with the excitement of the stick game, formed the Montreal Lacrosse Club. The Club, with atypical English decorum, ascribed boundaries, some rules, and together with earlier Indian refinements, gave justification to the claim that Montreal had thereby become the cradle of modem lacrosse.

The sport began spreading farther north of the Canadian-US border, into Ontario and Quebec. Several thousand spectators in 1860, including the Prince of Wales, witnessed a game between the Indians and the Montreal Lacrosse Club. The year 1867 was around the comer when Dr. Beers would get Parliament to take their defining action on the nation's game. Some of the more noteworthy rules passed included standardization of sticks, balls and goals. Teams were limited to twelve players per side. Touching the ball with hands, as in soccer, was anathema. The winner was the first to score three goals, although this was frequently amended by agreement or the setting of the sun.

The sport next began to trickle farther south over the border into upper-state New York. The Mohawk Lacrosse Club was organized in Troy, New York, shortly after Parliament's now suspect action in 1867, and was the first non-Indian club in the United States. Soon some prestigious colleges adopted the sport. They called the sport an inheritance from the "Noble Savage," in deference to the more pedestrian "Indians."

$$L$$

Although in 1870 New York University became the first US school to play lacrosse, by the late nineteenth century most of the Ivy League schools had begun playing. The Ivy imprimatur was a signal to exclusive private clubs to adopt teams. Thus, lacrosse began at the Boston Athletic Club, as well as at several New York clubs. Large athletic festivals were held in the late 1870s at the Westchester Polo Club in Newport, Rhode Island; at the New England Fair in Portland, Maine; and at the Ravenwood Lacrosse Club of Brooklyn, New York. Several thousand spectators all witnessed lacrosse matches at these festivals.

The Baltimore Athletic Club sent a track team to participate at a festival at Westchester, Rhode Island in 1878. They enthusiastically witnessed the lacrosse tournament. They were overwhelmed by the large boisterous crowd and the excitement of the game. The Brooks Brothers attired Baltimoreans, present at Newport, who were genteel and prosperous, purchased sticks and equipment which they brought back to Charm City. They determined to master the sport. A scant two months later, four thousand spectators turned out to watch these gentlemen athletes perform the first exhibition of lacrosse in Baltimore. The Baltimore Athletic Club in 1880 joined the young National Lacrosse Association, which had been formed in Ontario in 1867. It was comprised mostly of teams from New York, Quebec, and Ontario. The best teams were the Shamrock Club of Montreal and the New York Lacrosse Club.

The Baltimore Athletic Club in 1883 became the Druid Lacrosse Club because they played and practiced in Druid Hill Park. This field was near the campus of Johns Hopkins University. It was just a matter of time before the Hopkins students drifted over after chemistry or physics classes, borrowed or bought sticks, and began playing with the Druids. The genesis of the emergence of a lacrosse hotbed outside of the New York and Ontario axes were the Druids and Johns Hopkins University.

The emergence of another geographic focal point of the cultural history of lacrosse was British Columbia in Western Canada. The cities of Vancouver, New Westminster, and Victoria produced lacrosse clubs, and the competition of the teams nested the sport firmly in this western part of the Canadian landscape. British Columbia, like Ontario, had an appealing climate and economy, making the area a fertile field to plant lacrosse seeds. The New Westminster Salmonbellies' undefeated record against top eastern clubs in Ontario and Quebec in 1890 symbolized the national coming of age of lacrosse in British Columbia. A century later, Vancouver produced Paul and Gary Gait, who are considered to be among the all-time greatest players of the sport. They carried Syracuse to the NCAA championship over Loyola in 1990.

𝕃

Canadian lacrosse continued to thrive in Canada with the annual Mann Cup awarded to the winner of the East (Ontario) and West (British Columbia) competition. Clubs in these regions numbered several hundred. Then some European noblemen had a feud, which erupted into a global war called World War I. Canadian lacrosse never regained the relative level of popularity it had enjoyed during the late nineteenth century. When lacrosse players returned home from service in Europe, the old "national game" survived on the sporting landscape of Canada as a regionally bound sport, confined chiefly to southwestern British Columbia and southern Ontario. By the 1920s, baseball and softball dominated the sporting world in Canada.

L

In contrast to Canada, where lacrosse enjoyed a multi-class clientele, in the United States lacrosse attracted few followers from outside the affluent classes. In America it was "swells" from New York, New England polo players, lawn tennis snobs, and East River and Chesapeake Bay yachtsmen who made lacrosse part of their sporting portfolio. The seeds of lacrosse would germinate in New York, New England, and Baltimore, and the driving forces were the Ivy League and Johns Hopkins. Hopkins was founded in 1870, much later than the Ivy schools. Seven of the eight Ivy schools predate the American revolution. Only Cornell was founded later, in 1865, still before Hopkins. Johns Hopkins was and is an Ivy wannabee. Johns Hopkins University struggled to compete with the Ivy League marquee sports, especially football. But lacrosse was their equalizer. The powers at Homewood early on determined to indulge lacrosse where they could compete, defeat, and even dominate their Ivy League rivals.

Hopkins won its first of many inter-collegiate championships in 1891. Hopkins had picked up from the Druids a method of short passes, ball control, and running. This was in deference to the now discarded long passing game and it was the beginning of the carrying game. At the turn of the century, large crowds followed the sport and the growing number of teams, both college and club. But the game was becoming increasingly violent. It was characterized by flagrant, unnecessary roughness and fighting. The rules, such as they were, lacked the teeth necessary to control the game. The media, which was primarily newsprint, was repelled by the brutality and injuries, and began a covert boycott of coverage. Crowds dwindled. Many clubs and colleges dropped the sport. Then World War I cross checked lacrosse growth in the US much as it did in Canada.

Hopkins played an aesthetically pleasing game. Violence was not of their ethos. That and the emergence of the Mt. Washington Lacrosse Club saved the sport in the South. In the North, it was the Crescent Lacrosse Club of New York, which played the passing game and schooled its players against unnecessary violence. They actually modeled themselves after the clean style of game in Baltimore. The Crescents became a dominant force in New York for forty years.

The Druids lost their playing field in 1896, as the park was designated by a city ordinance to be a quiet park for citizens to wander about and feed the ducks in the lakes and soon pet the animals in the Baltimore Zoo. The Druids changed their name to the Maryland Athletic Club. But they were still referred to as the Druids for many years thereafter. And the ducks still lazily swim in the ponds of Druid Hill Park.

L

Hopkins was the inter-collegiate champion in 1897, 1898, and 1899. Hopkins had three injured players sent to the medical infirmary from the violence of an out of control Stevens's team in a game in 1900. Hopkins took a year's sabbatical from inter-collegiate lacrosse in the succeeding year. In the interim they played only clubs. In 1902, Hopkins was back and inter-collegiate champs again. They then defeated a strong University of Toronto team, five to two, before five thousand fans at Homewood. Toronto remained one of a few Canadian college teams among hundreds of Canadian club teams.

L

The Mount Washington Lacrosse Club was formed in 1904. They were sponsored by the Mt. Washington Cricket Club, which had an available field via an acquisition of a slice of property belonging to the tony Baltimore Country Club. It wasn't long before Mt. Washington edged the Druids for local supremacy. And the Wolfpack, as the Mounties were known, adopted the stylish play of the Druids and Hopkins.

L

The US Inter-collegiate Lacrosse Association was formed in 1905, although it was initially called the US Inter-collegiate Lacrosse League. A uniform code of rules was adopted. The years of 1907, 1909, and 1910, marked the initiation of the sport at Army, Navy, and Maryland respectively. The USILA was divided into northern and southern divisions. Hopkins began dominating the southern division and the Ivies the north. "Over here, over there, the Yanks are coming, the drums are rum-tumming everywhere", wrote George Cohan as World War I began. The Yanks included young lacrosse players, who traded playing fields for battle fields. So now war joined brutality as co-roadblocks on the path of the growth of the stick game.

At war's end in 1919, despite a new code of rules adopted by the USILA, rowdyism stained the Hopkins-Navy skirmish, sending multiple players from both teams to the penalty box and trainer's room. Rowdyism was still around, perhaps as a "substitute for war," the Indian mantra. It was a wound that wouldn't quite heal. The Indians were ironically playing a cleaner game in northern New York and southern

Ontario. Indians elsewhere had abandoned the game to riding the plains searching for the disappearing buffalo herds. The remaining Indian stickman formed their own clubs and adopted the American field lacrosse rules.

After their tough contest, Navy and Hopkins chose not to play each other for a while. Syracuse, in 1920 in up-state New York, began the sport that the Indians had played in their territorial backyard for decades. In the same year, St. Johns of Annapolis, in an attempt to emulate their cross-town rival Navy, began play. The sport flourished there until the onset of the second global war. After Pearl Harbor and the American entrance into the fray, St. Johns threw in the towel and abandoned all inter-collegiate athletics except for croquet, a serene and safe endeavor. Two players who had entered St. Johns to play lacrosse (as well as football), C. Mason "Daffy" Russell and Graham D. "Eggy" Russell, exchanged their sticks for rifles and joined the navy. They were my uncle and my dad. Daffy Russell is in the lacrosse Hall of Fame. He founded the sport at St. Mary's of Annapolis, an MIAA (formerly MSA) stalwart, and sent many players to D-I schools over his four decades of coaching. Also, up north, the state college of New Jersey, Rutgers, took up lacrosse in 1920.

In 1921, the USILA passed a formative rule in an attempt to soften the violence. Henceforth, at least three players and the goalie were required to remain behind the center line when the ball was being played on the other side of the center line. This was the stabilizing "off sides" rule. This seriously limited the unseen hand-to-hand combat of entire squads bunched around the goal or massive scrums for loose balls. A year later, face masks were made mandatory. It would now only be ice hockey players who smiled toothlessly.

𝕃

The Mt. Washington Club of the South and the Crescents of the North continued as exemplary ambassadors for the sport. They played each other annually, usually for the US Club or Open Championship. They played other clubs, mostly in Maryland and New York, and they played colleges up and down the East Coast. They energized the sport significantly in Maryland and New York. The Mounties began donating a cup to the Baltimore high school champion. High school lacrosse began in the United States in Baltimore shortly after the turn of the century. It was primarily private schools, most notably St. Paul's, Boys Latin, McDonogh, Severn, Friends, and Gilman. Poly and City soon became the first public schools to join the prep ranks. Today its successors are called the Maryland Independent Athletic Association, or MIAA. Its A Conference is considered the strongest prep lacrosse league in the USA, in no small way owing to its early start. This league became and remains a prime feeder for colleges, especially in Maryland. Loyola, regretfully, was not a beneficiary of this largess of talent until recent years.

L

In 1932, the Crescents lost their field in Brooklyn and moved to Long Island. The focus of lacrosse then shifted from metropolitan New York to Long Island, where it continues to this day. The Crescents were absorbed into the already existing Long Island Lacrosse Club. But as happened when the Druids changed their name and venue, the team continued to be called the Crescents for many years.

The Long Island Lacrosse Club was not as successful as Mt. Washington in getting lacrosse started in prep schools. But Maryland schools did have the head start, and a scant four miles from the Wolfpack field existed the finest lacrosse program in America, namely,

14

Johns Hopkins. The Long Island prep program did not really catch on until the 1950s. The prime catalysts were the fine program at Hofstra University and the Hofstra coach, Howdy Myers, from Baltimore and Johns Hopkins. Before Howdy sold lacrosse up and down Long Island, there were but five high schools playing. There are now literally hundreds in this very crowded metropolis they call Long Island. The Island has been solidly cemented and paved with roads, homes, schools, shopping centers, and parking lots. The remaining grass grows primarily on the playing fields and golf courses.

𝕃

Following the post-World War I peace, with the return of the young athletes from Europe, several other colleges embarked upon lacrosse programs. Among them were Washington College of Chestertown, Maryland and the University of Delaware in Newark, Delaware. As the crow flies, both schools are within eighty miles of the metropolitan area of Baltimore and have compiled rich lacrosse portfolios. Loyola's rich history was compiled well after these programs.

𝕃

Compared to the United States, in the early twentieth century Canada had a markedly different social footprint. Canadian lacrosse became embedded in local clubs with working class players who frequently banned together for ethnic reasons. The Shamrocks were Irish Catholic laborers. The Montreal LC were middle class Anglo Protestants. The American counterpart was found within institutions of higher learning. In America, lacrosse allowed the sons of affluent families to participate in a springtime alternative to the democratic and commercialized national pastime of baseball. Lacrosse in both clubs and colleges allowed the "gentlemen" players to cross sticks against members of the same affluent social class.

L

Into the thirties Canada adopted box lacrosse. The abandonment of field for box was quick and complete. Advocates started filling every empty ice hockey arena in southern Ontario, southwestern British Columbia, and Montreal in hockey's off season. They reduced the number of players to seven. Where an arena was unavailable, they built outdoor boxes. The Mann Cup became a box tournament between East and West. The first box Mann Cup was fought between the Hamilton Tigers and the Winnipeg Argos. Although the Great Depression and World War II reduced the number of teams, box lacrosse came back strong in the sixties. Even the Indians of Canada switched to box lacrosse. Today, the National Lacrosse League, with teams in thirteen cities in Canada and the US, is dominated by the Canadian players. I had the honor of being the first commissioner of the box league known as the MILL (Major Indoor Lacrosse league), which became the NLL. That was followed by several years as the general manager of the Baltimore Thunder. We were a successful franchise. We were always competitive and averaged 7,500 fans in the Baltimore Arena. New ownership bought the team in 1995 and hired their own staff. Within two years the team was gone. It bounced through a couple of cities before ending up in Colorado, where it still plays and is now owned by the Coors Brewing family. It leads the league in attendance, averaging fifteen thousand per game.

𝕃

During the first two decades of the twentieth century, college and club lacrosse grew slowly among well-to-do sportsmen in Baltimore and New York and among elite universities throughout the Northeast. And sportsmen of Johns Hopkins, Mount Washington, the Crescent AC, and the Ivy League all remained committed to the growth of the game. They all helped start prep school programs as feeders. But their programs did not turn to lower-class farmers and miners as the football counterparts did. Instead they turned to the affluent prep school boys with whom they shared common interests. Although early on football was also considered the preserve of the Northeastern elite, the elite sponsors of football were unable to contain its growth, and it soon rocketed from Yale and Harvard to Army, Navy, South Bend Indiana, Ohio, Michigan, and all the way west to the University of Southern California. The farmers and miners of the Midwest Ohio Valley and Northwest Pennsylvania have been surpassed by the southern players of the Bible belt. The latter play in the Southeastern Conference (SEC). College football was destined to conquer all of America. My son, Brendan, an Alabama alum, chants "Roll Tide Roll," as if it were a sacred Gregorian chant.

Donald Fisher, in his *History of the Game*, succinctly summarizes the sociological aspects of lacrosse as compared to football and baseball. "Like proponents of baseball and football, lacrosse supporters professed an ideology revealing the instrumental and symbolic functions they believed their game served. When enthusiasts in New York, New England, and Baltimore assessed lacrosse, they underscored a commitment to Victorian amateurism and the manly character-building qualities the sport allegedly inculcated." Fisher further crystalizes the Hopkins thing: "The students, coaches and alumni at Johns Hopkins hold special historical significance for their role in ensuring the prominence of lacrosse at the university." They appreciate the role of lacrosse as promoting the fame, fortune, and cultural leadership of the university. Furthermore, only well-to-do sportsmen felt secure enough about the alleged superiority of their race and class to associate themselves with Native Americans in any way. They ignored the fact that they appropriated the game from the Indians. But they conceded it was a "noble" theft. Its equestrian class supporters considered lacrosse as polo without horses.

L

As teams grew in the Northeastern corridor of the US, the USILA continued to use its influence to tame the violence. In 1932 they reduced the time of a match from two forty-five-minute halves without time-outs or substitutes to fifteen-minute quarters with timeouts and unlimited substitutions. They added playing space behind the goals. The on-field squad was reduced to ten from twelve. In the same year the USILA adopted a rule to make faceoffs safer. At the faceoff and before the referee blew the whistle, players, except the two parties facing off, were now to be restricted to wing areas for midfielders. And the remaining players were confined behind restraining lines near each goal. Prior to the new rule, everyone would be bunched around the center face-off circle like starved cannibals with clubs. Now the cannibals were restrained from mass clubbing, clawing, and clobbering.

Faceoffs for out-of-bounds balls were eliminated in 1935. After a shot, the ball was now awarded to the player nearest the ball when it went out of bounds. Otherwise the player last touching the ball would forego possession. The USILA was intent on taming the game, stemming violence, and adding civility and crowd appeal. The size of the playing field was reduced to its present dimensions of eighty yards between goals and fifteen yards behind the goals in 1940. And the width was conformed to be between sixty and seventy yards.

L

In the pre-World War II halcyon era, the Northeast corridor saw many new schools starting the stick game. Among them were MIT, Virginia, Lehigh, Washington and Lee, Duke, North Carolina, and the Loyola College Greyhounds of Baltimore, Maryland. Going into the war period, there were thirty-one colleges playing the game. All were located between New England and stretching along the East Coast south to North Carolina. The war predictably took its toll on lacrosse growth in America. As with the interruption of brutality at the turn of the century and then World War I, lacrosse play drastically declined. By the end of World War II, the number of colleges playing was fifteen. But the post-war boon pattern again accelerated the growth, and by 1949, fifty colleges were playing. In 1951, the rule-makers were still trying to legislate for civility and even beauty, plus speed and order. They decreed that body checking would be permitted only upon the player with the ball or upon a player without the ball if the ball is loose and if the targeted player is within fifteen feet of said loose ball. Thus, blocking and moving as flying picks, like the Green Bay Packer sweep, was forever ended. In 1948 the USILA prohibited throwing of the stick, a senselessly violent act frustrated participants had taken to. In the same year, the crease was changed from rectangular to circular, making for the smoother flow of traffic around the goal.

L

Post World War II, crowds were starting to pick up, with the rules promoting a safer, smoother game. Twelve thousand fans turned out for the Army-Navy game in Annapolis in 1949. A year later, fifteen thousand watched Navy beat Maryland, again in Annapolis. Hopkins and Maryland in Baltimore drew ten thousand. In the same year, seven thousand watched Syracuse and RIP in New York. By 1964, eighty-four colleges were playing lacrosse. Thirty had begun between 1952 and 1964. Some things were constant. Hopkins was still winning games, winning championships, and drawing big crowds to their Homewood field. Other Maryland schools, namely Navy, Maryland, and the University of Baltimore, all were building significant histories. Loyola had not yet emerged with a notable legacy; its primacy was still in its infancy. The Ivy League schools and Syracuse, Virginia, and Army also were among the preeminent institutions acquiring and cultivating their lacrosse histories. But Hopkins was still the leader.

L

No college has a lacrosse resume like Hopkins. Since lacrosse entered the Homewood campus, the Blue Jays have garnered forty-four national championships. The winner of the Maryland game gets a large wooden crab, which is "The Rivalry Trophy." Hopkins has many rivals. They have annual skirmishes with Syracuse, Virginia, and Princeton. They also play Loyola. Until recent years their game was known as "The Charles Street Massacre." It's so named because Loyola usually got massacred. It got so bad that after being perennially clobbered, Loyola withdrew from the series for twenty-four years. Hopkins has missed only one NCAA tournament since its inception in 1971. At Homewood, it was a series of very bright teachers who doubled as coaches who made the sport a cerebral as well as athletic endeavor. Some of their names were William Schmeisser, an attorney; Dr. Kelso Morrill; Bob Scott, long time coach and AD; and Henry Ciccarone, one of my Uncle Daffy's St. Mary's products. When these leaders were not teaching differential equations, Supreme Court decisions, micro-organisms and the like, they were refining the screen shot, the fast break, and extra-man play.

Hopkins joined the Big 10 in 2014 as an affiliate member for lacrosse. The Big 10 is a power conference for football and basketball. Hopkins won the initial Big 10 lacrosse tournament, beating Ohio State. Dave Pietramala, a former Hopkins All American, has been at the helm since the year 2000. He also played on our Thunder team, Baltimore's entrant in the MILL. Petro was like a player coach on the Thunder. I can still hear his booming voice ordering players, under penalty of his wrath, to not jump the boards onto the field until Russell said "Go." I was the GM, and John Stewart, my life- long friend, was the head coach. I would always work in the box during games and ran the subs in. Sometimes I needed help to control anxious players. Dave soon took a job as head coach of Cornell. His success there led to the Blue Jays job. And he has had continued success with the Jays.

Loyola's success would come too, but it was a long time coming. The darkest hour is always just before the dawn.

Playing the game created by "Noble Savages."

"Lacrosse looks like a real intellectual game to me. I expect to see somebody's brains knocked out, any minute now."

Will Rogers

CHAPTER TWO:

LACROSSE CONTINUES IN BALTIMORE

Other teams have made significant history in lacrosse in America. Many of those teams are geographically close to the Baltimore home of both Hopkins and Loyola. A storm was brewing at the US Naval Academy in Annapolis, Maryland in the early sixties. No one noticed the impending clouds, followed by a rainbow of bright wins. In 1959, Willis P."Bildy" Bilderback became the Navy coach. He was a legend and made an impact on the game to rival that of the many impactful contributions of Hopkins. Lacrosse began at the Naval Academy in 1908 when, predictably, two former Hopkins players volunteered to help form a team. Navy was undefeated in 1911. The 1917 season was cancelled because of World War I. But thereafter, Navy won forty-five consecutive games. The founder of the program at cross-city rival St. Johns, William "Dinty" Moore, assumed the reigns of the team in 1936. He remained at the helm for twenty-three years, during which time he helped Navy compile six national championships. Those two streaks of success would be surpassed by Bildy. A

Rutgers alumnus, he led Navy to eight consecutive national championships. His methodology revolutionized lacrosse and, ultimately, spurred rule changes.

In his initial season Bildy engineered an upset of national champion Hopkins. His team was coming. By the next year, they were practically unstoppable and remained unstoppable until the end of the decade when others began to emulate their technique. The secret to their success was patently obvious. But the Lords of Lacrosse, being close vested, traditionally Victorian, and slow to change, didn't see it. Bildy didn't need to recruit a plethora of stars from the prep leagues. Two or three good stick handlers would do. He had one named Jimmy Lewis, who remains an all-time great. He was Ervin "Magic" Johnson with the crosse and the shifty feet of Barry Sanders. For the remainder of the team, Bildy just recruited good athletes from the brigade and taught them how to play. He got large football players to play defense. He planted them around the goal like immoveable trees. When they slapped the ball out of an opponent's stick, they scooped it up and ran it down the field, where they made a quick flip to the Navy attackman. Rudimentary stick work sufficed. He didn't want a defenseman who played the position in high school. He reasoned that they only played high school defense because they were too slow to play elsewhere.

He would recruit athletic kids who had played in high school and make them better. They didn't need to be as great as Jimmy Lewis. Loyola High, now known as Loyola Blakefield, had just started their lax program in the late fifties. Owen McFadden and Dennis Wedekind were products of that young team which played in the MSA (now the MIAA) but only in the "B" division. Bildy made them All Americans at the Academy. Brian Lantier from Huntington High School on Long Island, not yet a New York power, became a three-time All American and Navy captain. He became a dear personal friend who passed two years ago after a long battle with cancer. Denny Wedekind and I stayed at his house overlooking the San Francisco Bay for the 2014 Americas Cup yacht races. Many of my lacrosse friends have remained friends for a lifetime. Owey McFadden was my golf partner in a tournament at the Shenvalee resort in New Market, Virginia in 2016. He is a veterinarian, having studied vet medicine after his naval tour of duty.

In deference to endless scrimmaging, Bildy spent countless hours on stick drilling and conditioning. They drilled repeatedly on passing while running. He made his players and the team super. Up to this time, most teams relied on two midfields. Some teams relied on but one midfield unit and occasionally took them out for a blow or wind break. Bildy began sending in three or four units, who were given orders to go full tilt, press their opponents all over the field as a Boston Celtics full court press, and then come out on the fly. The traditionalists finally figured Navy out. At the end of the decade, Maryland, and of course Hopkins, solved the simple riddle. They adopted the Navy style of run, run, hit, hit, check, check, with multiple midfields, and recruit a few good stickmen from the preppie ranks. But get good athletes on the field. And do constant drills and conditioning all during the school year and on summer leave. The conditioning was a requirement of every midshipman and a part of the curriculum at every service academy.

As a Loyola Hound, we traveled to Annapolis to scrimmage against one of these deep athletic Navy teams. It seemed as though they had a hundred players running all over the place. They were immaculately dressed for a practice game. They looked good and were good. Our Loyola team of probably twenty players were dressed like rag-tags in bargain basement practice uniforms. The Loyola athletic budget did not provide any frills for lacrosse. Sometimes we were short on balls, necessitating scavenger hunts for the white rocks hiding in the grass. We were intimidated and overwhelmed by Navy's relentless numbers. Not surprisingly, the Academy didn't ask us back the succeeding year. But we had a great dinner in the Navy dining hall. Navy probably felt that St. Paul's prep school would be a better practice opponent.

After Bildy left the Academy, Navy never won another national championship. The NCAA passed a rule several years later which quashed this style of play. They allowed two extra-long sticks on the field. Thence, teams looked to get two long sticks on the field when losing the ball, in deference to running in a whole new midfield. Many long for a return to the three defensemen, long stick days, and a faster game. The rule now allows four long sticks. Loyola played Navy in 1943 and suffered their third decisive loss against no wins. Mercifully, it was many years before the Hounds faced Navy again. They now play each other annually in the Patriot League. The Hounds hold an 8-4 record against the Midshipmen, losing only once in the modem era.

L

Navy is located forty miles south of Hopkins. Situated forty miles west of Hopkins is the University of Maryland. With the arrival of lacrosse on the Maryland campus in 1924, it wasn't long before an intense rivalry began between the Terps and Blue Jays. That game makes the Battle of Charles Street between Hopkins and Loyola pale in significance. However, the Greyhound loyalists make besting Hopkins akin to an appearance of the Virgin Mary on campus. Maryland has a history close to that of Hopkins. They have never had a losing season. They have amassed twelve national championships. Maryland and Hopkins have faced each other more than one hundred times. It is widely considered the greatest rivalry in college lacrosse. The Maryland program began as a club team in 1995. In Maryland's first year as a college sport, they snapped Navy's forty-six-game winning streak. In 1936 Maryland won the inaugural Wingate trophy, awarded to the USILA champion.

From the first USILA Terps team, they, along with Hopkins, Navy, and St. Johns, dominated college lacrosse for years, at least until World War II. All those schools are located in Maryland. Their success was due in large part to the high caliber of the sport in the Baltimore high schools. This included the private schools— many of which didn't field baseball teams in deference to lax in the spring—and the public schools, City and Poly. The importance of lacrosse in the community of Baltimore was magnified by the lack of any professional teams in the city until the creation of the Colts in 1947 and the return of the Orioles in 1954.

The US fielded an Olympic team as a demonstration sport in 1928 and 1932. Tournaments were held to choose who would represent the US. Maryland was in each tournament. In 1928, fifteen thousand fans watched Hopkins best Maryland in the finals to go to the Amsterdam Olympics. Four years later, Hopkins again bested Maryland to earn a trip to the Olympics in Los Angelos. Maryland was the 2017 NCAA National Champion. John Tillman has been at Maryland since 2011, and he directed the end of the drought of championships since 1975. That '75 team was coached by Clayton "Buddy" Beardmore, a three-time All American at Maryland. He was one of those midfielders who scarcely ever came out of a game. Buddy was my teammate on the old University Club Collegians. Later, Buddy was the GM of the Washington Wave of the MILL while I ran the Baltimore Thunder. He was a dapper, handsome man, who had two sons who became lax stars in their own right, one of whom played on the Thunder.

John Tillman, a Cornell grad, labored as an assistant at Navy for several years before becoming the head coach of Dartmouth. When

Dave Cottle stepped down as the Terps' coach, Maryland grabbed Tillman, a hot young candidate who was a steely genius who put Bill Belichick-type game plans together. He remains a bachelor and is reported to be married to lacrosse. He is a close friend of Charley Toomey, the Hounds' current coach. Maryland has had some great teams, players, and coaches over the years. Frank Urso, who played in the mid- 1970s, is one of just four college men's lacrosse players to be named a first-team All American all four years. Besides Tillman and Beardmore, other memorable coaches included Dr. Jack Faber, A1 Heagy, Dave Cottle—who left Loyola to coach at Maryland—and the late, beloved "Big Man" Dick Edell. Coach Edell also had successful stints at U of B and Army. As with Hopkins, Loyola avoided the powerful Terps for years. The series stood at 20-3 for Maryland in 2012 when Loyola beat the Terps in Foxboro for the NCAA championship.

The University of Baltimore fielded teams from 1949 through 1983, when they abandoned intercollegiate athletics altogether, much as St. John's did decades earlier. At that time, it was a small commuter college as Loyola, which is incidentally still small but no longer a commuter school. BU's success on the lacrosse field far exceeded that of Loyola during those years. At one time or another, the Bees, as they were called, defeated Syracuse, Harvard, Dartmouth, RPI, and Virginia. They played an ambitious schedule, which included Cornell, Penn, Loyola, Army, and Navy. "Big Man" Dick Edell coached the team from 1972-76. He won at least ten games every year. When the program was shut down in 1983, the coach was Ritchie Meade, who was later the coach at Navy.

Tall and lanky Randy Walker, whom the U of B recruited out of St. Paul's prep program, was one of the better middies of all time. The Bees' A1 Cosgrove outscored the great Jim Brown (from Syracuse and later the Cleveland Browns) in the 1957 USILA North–South game at Homewood, seven to five. BU, my law school alma mater, is located on North Charles Street in midtown Baltimore, three miles farther south on the same street as Hopkins. Stroll one- mile farther north from Hopkins and you find Loyola and their Evergreen campus. With so many colleges taking up the game today, it doesn't seem right that BU, with an undergraduate enrollment similar to Loyola, is still without a team. The boisterous crowds that filled the bleachers on the east side and sat on the stone wall on the west side of the Mt. Washington field are now sadly silent. The field is bereft of empty beer cans and is now a golf driving range. BU was a career 15–5 versus Loyola.

𝕃

Heading farther up Charles Street, about four miles north of Loyola, and taking a right turn at Towsontowne Boulevard will lead you into Towson University. There is the campus of the second largest school in the state. It is among the larger state universities in the country, with twenty thousand undergrads and three thousand grad students. The Towson Tigers began lacrosse play in 1958. They started slowly, as our Greyhounds gave them a good shellacking in their initial encounter in 1960. In a few short years the trend was reversed. Towson rapidly became a power in D-II of the NCAA. They won the National D-II championship in 1974. That team featured All Americans Jimmy Darcangelo and Bob Griebe. Bob and I were the initial coaches of the Baltimore Thunder of the MILL. Bob was the head coach and I was his only assistant. I remember vividly our initial game at the Baltimore Arena, played before 8,500 fans on a Saturday afternoon. Bob had been called out of town by his employer, and I was left to run the team by myself. All involved in this new pro venture had other employment, and our participation in pro box lacrosse was a part-time avocation. Behind the faceoffs of Steve Stenersen, the long-time CEO of US Lacrosse, the hustle of Chuck Muir from BU, Peter Jenkins from Delaware, and "Darky" Darcangelo, we bested the Philadelphia Wings in overtime. The coach of the Wings was Dave Huntley from Hopkins. Dave congratulated me, then deadpanned, "How much did you bribe the refs?!" I am all but certain he was kidding.

Towson soon moved up to D-I and has been a constant force among the major college lacrosse elite. They have made fourteen NCAA tournament appearances. They made it to the championship game in 1991, where they fell to North Carolina, 18–13. They play their games in the largest college stadium in metropolitan Baltimore, Johnny Unitas Stadium, with a seating capacity of eleven thousand. It took Loyola a while to catch up to Towson, but their annual battles are always close and hard fought. I taught an early morning business law class at Towson as a young lawyer and obtained my master's degree in liberal arts from there. The school has an abundance of programs, both athletic and academic. Its expansive campus of classic red brick colonial architecture pleasingly blends in with the adjoining neighborhoods. Towson U is situated south of the Towson government center, while the little Ivy League school of Goucher anchors the north. Towson has become a true college town. The Hounds lead the Tigers in the overall series 33-28.

L

Southwest of Baltimore, just outside of the Beltway, lies a young school, UMBC, which was founded in 1966. The code name is short for the University of Maryland at Baltimore County. Schools seem to like code names. How about UCLA, USC, UCF, or The U (Miami)? But unlike UMBC, those schools have only men's club lacrosse teams. UMBC quickly became a leading research institution and yearly earns a high mark in the ratings of colleges and universities. Its sports teams are called the Retrievers, a name which hearkens to the Chesapeake Bay retriever, legendary helper to the hunters, anglers, and crabbers, who ply their sport and trade around the Bay environs. UMBC has achieved success on the lacrosse field. And, as with Towson, they initially dominated Loyola. The Hounds eventually turned around the series, once Loyola solidly entered D-I. Because UMBC plays in the America East Conference, they have not been matched against Loyola for a few years. Loyola, of course, has its own conference commitments in the Patriot League, in which nine of the ten conference schools field men's lacrosse teams. UMBC faces some formidable opponents in their conference. Included among those teams are the Albany Great Danes, another legendary dog that ran swiftly into the final four in 2018 before falling to Yale in the semis. To finish the canine connection, Yale's mascot is a bulldog. Perhaps UMBC's greatest athletic achievement occurred in the NCAA basketball tournament in 2018, wherein they upset number-one seed Virginia.

As with Loyola and Towson, UMBC spent productive years in D-II before moving up to D-I in 1981, two years before Loyola made the move. Also, as Towson and Loyola, UMBC reached the D-II championship game. In 1979 they were runner ups before winning the D-II title in 1980. In 1981, Loyola played in the championship and lost to Adelphi, 17–14. Dick Watts started the first UMBC team in 1968. The Retrievers did not fully fund their lax program until 1993, when they increased their scholarship allotment from 8 to the NCAA D-I max of 12.6. They immediately became more competitive, although they always played well under Watt's tutelage. Dick Watts retired that year and was succeeded by Don Zimmerman, who had previously coached at Hopkins and had won three national championships. Of course, that's what Hopkins does. UMBC won conference championships eight times. They have made six D-I tourney appearances. As with their basketball team, the laxers have won some great upsets, including wins over Maryland in 1998 and 2007. One of their early stars was Jeff Hahn, older brother of Greyhound star Scott Hahn. The younger Hahn was one of my recruits from Loyola High and one of my all-time favorite players. He was smallish but had a huge heart. In 2016, Loyola University Assistant Ryan Moran took over as head coach of the UMBC Retrievers lacrosse program. UMBC holds a lifetime 16–15 edge over Loyola.

L

The game of lacrosse underwent unprecedented change and growth in the seventies era. Since the inception of the game in the new world, all sticks were produced by the Indian tribes in Canada. The skilled Native Americans could only produce a finite number of sticks. As more teams began playing on both sides of the US–Canada border, the resources of stick production were seriously strained. The W. T. Burnett Company of Baltimore, producer of urethane foam used in the manufacture of insulation, furniture, and blankets, had opened a subsidiary in the Baltimore suburb of Timonium early in 1970. The subsidiary was called STX, Inc., manufacturer and producer of an adiprene stick, more commonly known as a plastic stick. These sticks could be mass produced, were lightweight, perfectly balanced, and had replaceable parts for easy repair. Within a year's time, the wooden stick, like the buffalo herds, was history. And the Indians in Ontario, who lovingly carved and wove lacrosse sticks, were now making tee-pees—or collecting wampum in the unemployment line.

The plastic stick has become a tremendous catalyst for the growth of the sport. Soon STX would have competition. Brine, Warrior and Maverik, among others, would quickly enter the market. They needed to pay STX a royalty, as STX had the US Patent. But now sticks were everywhere and teams from youth leagues to high schools to colleges exploded all over the United States. By the eighties, it wasn't just the hotbeds of New York and Baltimore producing premium lacrosse players. Hotbeds sprang up in Colorado, Connecticut, New Jersey, North Carolina, Georgia, Virginia, Pennsylvania, and many other pockets across the United States. The sport had moved well beyond its coastal prep school confines. It is estimated by Sports and Fitness Industry Association that 2.2 million Americans picked up a lax stick in 2017. The impact of the plastic sticks was immediate, expediting the social and geographic expansion of lacrosse throughout all of North America. Not only were the new sticks easier for manufacturers to market to consumers, but they made learning the game much easier.

Prior to STX entering the stick market, 95 percent of the sticks bought by Americans and Canadians came from the same manufacturer in Canada. It was known as the Chisholm Lacrosse Manufacturing Company. They sold their sticks directly to teams journeying to the factory reservation or to two sporting goods wholesalers. They were Bachrach Rasin of Baltimore and the W. H. Brine Company of Boston. In the 1960s it was important to get to the Bachrach's store downtown early enough, before practice began in February, to get a balanced stick. With the arrival of the plastic stick, other dealers entered the market. Jimmy Darcangelo was on the sales force of Bachrach. He resigned to begin his own company, LAX World, with partner, Lance Holden. Bachrach soon brought suit against Darky to enjoin him from using his Bachrach contacts to expand his new business. I represented Darky, and we were able to settle the matter, thanks to the cooperation and negotiating skill of Bachrach's fine young attorney, Herb O'Connor, a former player at Boy's Latin and Villanova. And fortuitously, Herb was one of my best friends. It wasn't long before multiple lacrosse equipment companies emerged and Bachrach's was gone, like the wooden sticks. Lance passed away, but Darky had great success, and Lax World eventually had ten stores nationwide before selling to a group of loyal employees. A sad footnote is that Lax World eventually followed the fate of Bachrach's and succumbed to multiple competitors.

The plasticization of sticks allowed for greater access to the sport by less affluent enthusiasts. By the late nineties, other companies, most notable of which was Warrior Lacrosse, had designed and introduced lighter sticks with titanium shafts. The wooden handle was now gone too. In the end, modem industrial capitalism had triumphed over a traditional native craft. The game had become a faster game. But the unseen subtle change was that the sport no longer was the exclusive property of an elite part of America, most visible in the Ivies and Hopkins. No longer were the best players those who were born with a silver stick in their mouths. Don Fisher sums up the resultant changes in the sport as follows: "Many new to the game, lower middle-class and working-class people, suburbanites, African Americans, corporations such as Toyota, and people residing in places far from the Northeast did not accept as intact the elite amateur values of the 'old Indian game.'" My brother-in-law, Ramsey Flynn, wrote perceptively in Baltimore magazine of the status of lacrosse in the eighties, which would evaporate in the nineties. He said of parents watching their children carry on the family tradition of lacrosse: "You're not going to see any parents out there in bowling shirts." Rather they were all gathered in clusters of "Kelly green or Oxford blue." He further said that lacrosse in Baltimore had traditionally been a Blue Book sport. But now the masses clamored for inclusion, and they would have their way.

𝕃

The Lacrosse Foundation was established in 1959, with headquarters on the Johns Hopkins campus. Where else! They embarked on an ambitious plan to expand the game. In the 1980s, the Foundation launched a youth program for urban African Americans. This augmented their existing programs, which not only evangelized the sport through their magazine, but provided start-up equipment to youth groups throughout the country. The Lacrosse Foundation became US Lacrosse in 1997. Soon every lacrosse organization, including the US Women's Lacrosse Association, coalesced under their umbrella. Steve Stenersen became the permanent Executive Director. He placed a high priority on middle-class suburbanites, inner-city youth, and other sportsmen and women outside of the Northeast. The notion of lacrosse as a game only for gentleman, played on elite fields, was dead.

Lacrosse ceased to be racially homogeneous in 1969, as the predominately black Morgan State University took up the sport. They were coached by Chip Silverman, another one of my teammates on the University Collegians Club team. We usually sat on the bench together, wishing for a big lead so we would be sent in with the scrubs. In 1975, the Morgan Bears upset Washington and Lee, a top- rated team full of Baltimore preppies. Chip recalled, "They never got over that loss. A bunch of blacks went down there and beat them at their game." Regretfully, the black athlete never fully embraced lacrosse as their sport of choice because football, basketball, and baseball, unlike lacrosse, offered them economic benefits. Jim Brown, of the NFL and movie fame, always said that lacrosse was his favorite sport, but it didn't pay " much scratch."

𝕃

A few short years after the shocking W & L upset, lacrosse had left the Baltimore campus of Morgan. Due to budget constraints and the advent of Title IX, the sport was dropped in 1981. In the mid-seventies, many college players participated in a summer league in Baltimore known as the Heroes league. Chip's assistant, Sheldon Freed, coached one of the six teams, and it was predictably manned by several Morgan Bears. Chip called me and advised that Sheldon's dental school responsibilities had forced him to resign as the summer league coach. Chip asked me if I could take over. I did so with relish, and we went undefeated until the title game. We lost to a team coached by Dave Cottle, eventual Loyola coach. Dave at that time was still an undergrad at Salisbury. He was testing his coaching mettle and came up positive.

I still have fond memories of those athletes from Morgan, most of whom I remember well. I think wistfully of that summer with Dink Brown, Tyrone Scott, Aaron Glover, George Kelley, and others. The latter, George Kelley, was a very smart person and player who, after four years as an Army officer, became a policeman in Baltimore City. He retired after twenty years and then continued in uniform as a deputy sheriff in Baltimore County. When I would run into him in the courthouse, he would give me a strong "Bear" hug.

During the title game a number of fights broke out, and I was arguing with the referees about some questionable calls. Several opposing players surrounded me quite closely. George came to the rescue, laying out four guys before I advised, "George, that's enough. I think we made our point!" Dave Cottle stood with his arms folded, waiting for another referee call, which resulted in reciprocal unsportsmanlike penalties. I think it was worth the penalty. This incident made it to

Chip's memorable book *Ten Bears*. It was the story of the Morgan State Bears lacrosse team and was made into an ESPN film. Chip was a colorful guy who wore an afro, mutton chop sideburns, and seventies hip clothes, including bell bottoms. Those styles disappeared with the Morgan team. At Loyola, as the Morgan team was starting to fade and Loyola was starting to rise, we played the Bears over three seasons and won easily. But the total series stands at 5–5, owing to the strong initial years of the Bears. Actually, the Bears demise began after Chip retired in 1976 to give full attention to his job as Maryland State Drug Administrator. The title of this project is a fond nod to Chip, who departed too young.

As a footnote to my friendship with Chip, he was an original member of the young men who were the inspiration for the movie *Diner Boys,* a Barry Levinson classic film. It was about some kids from Forest Park High School who hung out at a diner in northwest Baltimore. Chip grew up with Levinson and frequently assisted him with screen writing and editing. He helped occasionally with Levison's TV show *Homicide*, which was filmed in Baltimore. Chip created a character in the series who was a public defender named Russell Darrell. I received no royalties.

The NCAA had tournaments for all of their sports except Division I-A in football and in lacrosse. Football leaders resisted because of the proliferation of lucrative bowl games. A consortium of major bowls banded together and created a four-team playoff in 2014. After years of picking the national lacrosse champion, which was awarded the Wingate trophy, the lords of Lacrosse succumbed to NCAA pressure. No longer would the committee elect a champ by vote. Some previous votes were very controversial. In 1957 the committee awarded the championship to—and here's a surprise—Hopkins, in a narrow vote over undefeated and Jim Brown–led Syracuse. In 1967 the vote produced a three-way tie, between Navy, Hopkins, and Maryland, leaving most very unhappy. In 1971 the inaugural tournament was held among eight teams. Cornell, of the Ivies, won this tournament. As the years passed and as the number of lacrosse-playing schools mushroomed, the number of tournament entries was increased. Tournaments were added in succeeding years to Divisions II and III. Initially all teams were divided into either the University division or the College division, thereby separating big schools from smaller schools. A tournament was established for the College division in 1972. By 1973 the NCAA wrestled control from the lords and legislated all lacrosse playing schools into Divisions I, II, and III. This mirrored all the college sports except D-I football. All three divisions would have season-ending tournaments, for men's and women's lacrosse. Finally!

In 2018 there are 73 D-I men's lacrosse programs. There are 61 playing D-II. And there are 236 D-III programs. Here's a surprise to some. The women have surpassed the men in college programs. There are 112 schools that have D-I women's teams and 106 that have D-II teams. And in D-III, an astounding number, 282, play. Women's lacrosse had a beginning not necessarily parallel to the men. Unlike the men, who found their lax roots in Baltimore and New York, the women began organized play in Philadelphia. However, the first women's team was Bryn Mawr of Baltimore in 1926. Needless to say, the growth of women's lacrosse has also spread across the land. There are many reasons why there are more women's than men's teams. Primarily it is a simpler game with less equipment. Its rules are very stringent for defensive play, clearly making the women's version a non-contact sport. Any check must be well below the helmetless head.

The check must be stick on stick and should the stick touch skin, a penalty shot will ensue.

Title IX has been a constant inhibitor of men's college lacrosse growth. Title IX was the 1972 Equal Opportunity in Education Act passed by Congress. In summary, it prescribes that any college receiving any federal funds, directly or indirectly (which is most schools), must give the same amount of aid to women's sports as to men. To do otherwise is discriminatory. The legal efficacy of the act was confirmed in the 1988 Supreme Court case of Grove City College v. Bell. If the college or university has a football team with eighty rides, the schools must give a corresponding eighty rides to women athletes. For example, in the PAC 12 in the West, almost all schools field women's NCAA lacrosse teams, but none field men's teams. That is why lax has proliferated in D-III. There are no athletic scholarships, per se, in D-III. Finally, for all those colleges who do not have varsity lacrosse, men or women, there are club teams. There are 184 men's teams playing in the MCLA (Men's Collegiate Lacrosse Association). There are 225 women's colleges playing in the WCLA (Women's Collegiate Lacrosse Association).

There is a continuing negative feeling about the structure of the playoffs and the requirement that all games be scheduled with an awareness that the games must be completed at least two weeks before Memorial weekend, when the men's finals are played in all three divisions. Most teams in the three divisions play in conferences which have their own playoffs at season's end. After those games have transpired, at least two more weeks must be allowed for the elimination playoffs leading up to final four weekend. Thus, all competitive teams begin practice at the beginning of the spring semester, which is usually early January. Anyone who lives in the Northeast knows that in January and February, snow is all but inevitable. And practice on a winter white field is like skating on an icy tundra or sludging through mounds of drifted snow. Gone are the days when practice began in late February and the season was played into June on warm, sunny spring days.

Schools with generous athletic budgets have an advantage. Many such schools have indoor dome facilities. An advantage that Loyola has over local lax programs, including Hopkins, is an inflatable dome to keep its players toasty warm and dry. They check their LL Bean snow shoes at the door. Navy and Maryland, among local schools, also have indoor practice facilities. Loyola built its inflatable dome with funds from four anonymous donors. I've been sworn to secrecy as to the identity of the mysterious benefactors, under penalty of losing my skybox pass.

L

So, there have been three threads that have pushed lacrosse into mainstream America, away from the narrow confines of the Northeast elite. Firstly, it was technology and the production of the plastic stick and safer helmets and lightweight protective equipment, which made the game available to middle America. Then it was the egalitarian, democratic ethos of the Lacrosse Foundation, which became US lacrosse and successfully evangelized the sport to a diverse citizenry. It utilized print and social media and an outreach program which gave equipment and coaching to all parts of the US. Finally, it was the NCAA, which seized the game from the stodgy, elite lords by creating a structure of playoffs which made the sport exceedingly more competitive and fun.

The weekend of Memorial Day has become an annual ritual called championship weekend. For the first twenty years or so, the D-I tournament used the college venue for all the games. The format remains the same. That is, the teams picked by the NCAA committee play an elimination series on college campuses. The D-I semi-finals are now played in an NFL stadium on the Saturday before Memorial Day with the final on Memorial Day Monday. On Sunday the finals are held in the same stadium for the D-II and D-III finalists. Despite ESPN coverage of the D-I semis and finals, the crowds at these professional venues have been tremendous. Loyola traveled to Foxboro in 2012 to play the final four games. They emerged victorious over this weekend, and a total of over sixty thousand attended for both days. This included a large contingent from Loyola Baltimore, which traveled up the East Coast by car, bus, train, and plane. The TV announcer proclaimed Loyola fans the best travelers in the lacrosse nation. Lacrosse had become their school's showcase sport. It wasn't always so. Hopefully, in these pages we can trace the long, steep climb of this little school from Baltimore to the mountaintop of the Lacrosse world.

Mark Donovan wrote in *Sports Illustrated* several years ago: "Today's lacrosse players and coaches sometimes romanticize about the old-fashioned boundary-less game the Indians played. It must have been savage, majestic, and free. But lacrosse devotees don't get too wistful about the good old days. They claim the modern game, more confined though it is, combines the best elements of football, hockey, soccer, and basketball. The hitting is hard and clean. The passing crisp and accurate. The running exhilarating and exhausting. All in all, lacrosse is one heck of a sport." And a few years earlier Alan Goldstein wrote in the *Baltimore Sun*: "Maryland was the mecca of lacrosse, a land of plenty with Baltimore as its hub, producing an endless supply of multi-talented big stars who assured national dominance year after year for Johns Hopkins, Maryland, Navy, and an occasional intruder from neighboring Virginia. It was a bigger monopoly than General Motors (bless their heart) ever envisioned." Alas, if Alan were writing today, he would have to add Loyola University Maryland to that storied list of schools which have attained national dominance and lacrosse immortality.

Chief Tecumseh: Looking for the creator's game at the Naval Academy

"It was in the colleges and universities rather than at the secondary-education level that problems were acute. Jesuits were not used to running big schools."

Peter McDonough

CHAPTER THREE:

THE JESUITS AND LACROSSE

It is universally accepted that as early Jesuit missionaries traversed America converting the Indians, they observed them doing their recreational thing of playing lacrosse. The Jesuits noted that the primitive sticks resembled a bishop's crozier, that is, his crosse. As it was the creator's game to the Indians, it had to be the voice of God that told the Jesuits to call the game La Jeu de la Crosse. To Americans and eventually Native Americans also, the game became simply lacrosse. St. Ignatius Loyola, together with six other young men, including St. Francis Xavier, in 1534, gathered and professed vows of poverty, chastity, and obedience to the Pope in matters of mission assignment and direction. Ignatius Loyola, a Basque nobleman from the Pyrenees area of northern Spain, founded the Society after discerning his spiritual vocation while recovering from a wound sustained in the Battle of Pamplona. Ignatius's plan of the new order's organization was approved by Pope Paul III in 1540.

Both Loyola Blakefield and Loyola University Maryland have statues of Ignatius Loyola in mid campus. The Loyola Blakefield statue depicts him kneeling with his sword in outstretched hands. He is presenting the sword upon the altar of the Chapel of Our Lady of Montserrat. He would henceforth be God's soldier, and the Jesuits would be God's soldiers or God's marines. It reflects the Society's commitment to accepting orders anywhere, which eventually would be the new world of America, populated by settlers and Native Americans. It was in the seventeenth century that the Jesuits would first come to America to convert, counsel, and educate. They fearlessly traveled everywhere to reach both Native Americans as well as settlers.

The Jesuits were relentless in putting their educational stamp on America. The tradition has propelled them to start and maintain twenty-eight colleges and universities in the United States. There are sixty-one high schools. But, as with all of Catholic clergy, the Jesuit numbers have declined in recent years. As a result, as of 2018, fifteen of the twenty-eight Jesuit universities in the U.S. have non-Jesuit lay presidents. The number of Jesuit priests who are active in the everyday operation of the schools is not nearly as high as it once was. But the conception of the mission of these schools remains a constant. It proposes Christ as the model of human life, the pursuit of excellence in teaching and learning and training men and women for others. This credo has impacted the sports programs of Loyola Maryland. But it manifests itself as a conundrum of sorts. Jesuit personnel are in the classrooms but rarely on the athletic fields. And they are rarely in administration.

Jesuits tend to see themselves primarily as teachers and character builders. The chores of administration and organization left them with little time for creative, positive gain in these areas. So, it was predictable that the Jesuits, who ran Loyola Maryland, never quite grasped the impact of lacrosse in the boardrooms of Baltimore. Consequently, for years Loyola was mired in abject mediocrity on the lacrosse field. At the same time, the southern powers of Hopkins, Navy, Maryland, Virginia, U of B, Washington College and the northern

Ivies, Army, and Syracuse were indulging their lacrosse programs to capture the collective approval of their alumni communities. Lacrosse success translated into generous legacies from alum supporters to the campus treasuries. But the Jesuits kept teaching excellence in the classrooms and prayed and hoped for a few victories on the field, where the students were coached by lay persons.

L

The college model depended on the perpetuation and generosity of traditional Catholicism, which was entering into decline in the late twentieth century. The financial productivity of the alumni community was more reflective of endowments, which often were beyond the Jesuits reach. This model worked at some of the smaller Jesuit schools, but those seeking a bigger-scale model plunged ahead and recruited a lay community of leaders to market the schools to increased size and solvency. And the Jesuits continued to stay in the classrooms and teach excellence and moral values. In the 60s at Loyola, the hierarchy of the Board and administration was becoming dominant with lay persons including the appointment of the first lay Chairman of the Board.

The Board named Fr. Joseph Sellinger as the President of Loyola in 1964. He was at that time a Dean at Georgetown University. He was a unique leader and not a typical Jesuit priest. He was Jesuit-wise of course, being a teacher of advanced chemistry. But his leadership skills took him from the classroom to the president's chair. There he became a politician. He inherited a campus of about one thousand commuters. He soon was building dormitories named after their benefactors, to wit, Butler and Hammerman Halls. He absorbed Mt. St. Agnes College in 1971. Loyola would soon buy much surrounding property, including all nearby apartment complexes, which would be converted to dorms.

When Fr. Joe assumed the presidency of Loyola College, as it was then called, the prime feeder of students came from north Baltimore city and county. Today it is still north, but it is northeast to New Jersey, New York, Connecticut, Massachusetts, and beyond, into the whole Northeast corridor. The student population has quadrupled to 4,000 undergrads and 1,800 grad students. At least 3,000 students are residents on campus. Yet it is still the smallest school to win an NCAA D-I lacrosse championship. And the Sellinger School of Business and Management is a lasting testimony to Fr. Joe's legacy. That and the NCAA D-l lacrosse title of 2012 watched by Fr. Joe from his celestial box seat. He was President until his death in 1993.

L

In 1852 Loyola College opened its doors on Holiday Street in Baltimore under the tutelage of Rev. John Early, the first president. Presently, if a donor gives at least $1,852 annually, he becomes a member of the John Early Society and is invited to a posh cocktail party with prime rib and oysters washed down by Grey Goose and Makers Mart. He also gets invited to the skybox at Ridley Stadium for big lax games. In 1855 the school moved up to Calvert and Madison Streets, the present site of St. Ignatius Loyola Academy and Center Stage. In 1921 the college moved to its present Evergreen campus in north Baltimore. Now amassing eighty developed acres, it was then a leafy but scruff oasis of trees, shrubs, and wild grass on perhaps twenty acres. Only one building existed on the tract of land purchased from the Garrett estate, the founding family of the B & O Railroad. It was the

Tudor-styled home of one of the Garrett children. It became the Jesuit residence and is now the Humanities Center.

The land awaited the surveyor's measure of its rolling contours of earthen dirt. Then the shovels and picks made way for the craft of the stone masons. What was produced was an ordered symmetry of flag stone buildings, which were given names of notable Jesuits: Wheeler Hall, Xavier Hall, and Beatty Hall. Jenkins Hall was named after a wealthy benefactor. The Alumni chapel would come later in 1952. It was designed to resemble the Jesuit Church of Gesu in Rome. All the buildings were designed as Collegiate Gothic Architecture. An athletic field was carved out east of the buildings. It was, encircled by a dirt track. Soon the field and track were filled with runners and football and baseball players. North of the field an adjacent gym rumbled with bouncing basketballs and happy shoes on the wooden floor. A mile south of Evergreen, the Homewood campus of Hopkins sat smugly and empirically. Lacrosse players grew like weeds at Homewood. They were nowhere to be found at Evergreen. That would change in 1938, when a handful of students pressured for a team. What followed were years of unremarkable mediocrity.

L

The first five Loyola Lacrosse teams were coached by Jack Kelly from 1938 through 1942. He had been an All-American goalie at Maryland. His teams won twenty-two and lost sixteen. Emil G. "Lefty" Reitz, Jr. was a caretaker coach for 1943. He was the AD, and Kelly had left for the war. Lefty, while also coaching baseball, babysat the laxers to a lackluster 1–4 record. Sports, including lacrosse, were shut down the next two years because of World War II and the diminishing number of students, as hordes left to battle the Axis powers. After the war, Bill Zeigler fared no better than his predecessors as he compiled a 1–3 record. Bishop Baker held the coaching reigns for the next six years. He had but two teams with winning records. Bish Baker, Jr. played on our teams in the early sixties. He was a scrappy player but fared better as a member of the wrestling team. He played close attack, and it was amusing to watch him try to wrestle crease defensemen. He was clever too, as he would stealthily hold the end of the defenseman's stick, unseen by the ref. Then the defenseman would retaliate with a furious penalized push, shove, or haymaker.

The records of the early teams are deceptive. The initial season had the Hounds playing four "B" teams. They actually beat the Hopkins "B" team twice and lost to the Maryland and Navy "B" teams. In 1939 the pattern began of losing big to strong teams. St. Johns, Hopkins, and Navy pummeled them, 14–4, 20–1, and 14–4, respectively. The following four years of play, prior to the World War II shut down, Navy, Maryland, and Hopkins continued winning big. Otherwise, Loyola held their own against lesser programs, similar to Loyola, such as, Lehigh, CCNY, Springfield, and W & L. This pattern continued after the war with huge losses to the traditional strong teams and parity with schools similar to Loyola.

John Mohler was another caretaker coach for the year of 1953, compiling a scintillating record of 2–4. Thereafter, the era of Charles "Batman" Wenzel began. He coached for seventeen years, and the mediocrity continued with the exception of a few bright moments and the occasional presence of some good players. Charley was a school teacher at Mergenthaler Vocational Technical high school located on Hillen Road in northeast Baltimore. Mervo, as it was known, had some tough kids. Charley would leave daily after classes at Mervo and head to Loyola, where the kids showed him respect and listened to him teach the art of scooping the ball with both hands. He didn't need to throw erasers to get their attention. Charley had played lacrosse at Maryland as a defenseman. All of Loyola's coaches were part-time except for the AD and the basketball coach. Basketball had always been king at Loyola. I don't know how much Charley was paid at Loyola, but it couldn't have been much. He survived for so long despite only five winning teams because the Loyola leadership didn't care, and Charley loved the job. I know what I got paid as an assistant coach at Loyola five years after Charley was gone. It was the magnificent sum of five hundred dollars for four months of practices and games. I did get a windfall of sorts in the fall when I coached cross country. I was paid the munificent sum of one thousand dollars. Over my six years of coaching at Loyola, I accumulated a kingly sum. It was enough for a vacation to exotic Middle River!

Batman was the name his players affectionately gave Charley. He had poor vision and wore thick glasses. Thus, he was blind as a bat, hence "Batman!" He wife was named Honey. I never knew whether that was her Christian name or what Charley called her. She came to every game and rode on the bus with us to away games. Charley and Honey had one child, Charles Wenzel, Jr. He was called Chuckie. He was a likeable little kid but was also kind of a nuisance. He came on the bus trips too. Charley and Honey would have died had they known all the abuse Chuckie got from certain players. A prime perpetrator was Marty Pilachowski, whom we called "Maurice de Pilla Hog," from his propensity to add girth. I can still picture Marty hanging Chuckie out of the bus window way in the back where the parents couldn't see. Chuckie thereafter ventured to the rear of the bus with great trepidation.

Marty was a typical player of this era. He was a good athlete from Loyola High. He had been a quarterback on the football team at the high school. He played a little bit of lacrosse at Loyola High but was not an accomplished player. But he fit in very well at the college simply because of his natural athletic ability. There were a lot of Martys.

Another noteworthy player was Lou Becker, also from Loyola High. He had an undistinguished high school career but became an immediate starter at the college and did quite well. Lou became a state judge, as did I. Perhaps the classic player was Michael Abromaitis. He also came from Loyola High, but there was no team there when he attended. He had fairly good stick work because many kids in his neighborhood played on private school teams like Boys Latin and Gilman, and he played a lot of catch and pickup games with them. Mike played a good attack at the college and was very solid. Mike's wife, Dr. Carol "Sue" Abromaitis, still teaches at Loyola in the English department. Mike and Sue have been very generous to the lacrosse program. Mike is a top-notch tax-business attorney. We each got in trouble for belonging to an illegal fraternity on campus called ZHO. It was certainly the only time model student, Mike Abro, ever got in trouble. I can make no such boast.

𝕃

Prior to the installation of lacrosse at the Catholic high schools—namely, Loyola, Calvert Hall, Mt. St. Joe, Curley, Gibbons, St. Mary's, and John Carroll—Loyola College had very few players who took the field with any high school experience. This caused the program from its inception to the early sixties to be a wasteland of sorts. Every now and then the team would come up with a good player who adapted quickly and became a standout, despite no secondary school experience. Some of those players were Don Litz, Bob McElroy, Jerry Courtney, John Mohler, and Ray Whittelsbereger, all of whom were post war players. Actually, Ray did play lacrosse at City. Occasionally someone would show up with the public school background. But Loyola didn't get the private preppie kids. They went to the Ivies, Hopkins, or an exclusive Virginia school.

Frank Kimmel, Tom Wagner, Bob and Ed Miller and Marty Barry of the early 1950s and Mickey McFadden and Jim Kelley of the late 50sera were standouts. But, as far as can be determined, they had no high school experience. And there were others who became good players. Jim Kelly had never seen a lacrosse game before he tried out at Loyola. By senior year he was selected to the North-South All Star game and was honorable mention All American. With the lacrosse programs flourishing at the Catholic schools, the college began getting players with experience. A lot of good players from Loyola High would start to appear on the Evergreen campus. During my 60s era we got a bonus of Marty Pilsch from City, who came to Loyola as a swimmer. Page Fried and Jim Norton arrived from Poly, and Harry Bregel and Jack and Dennis Palmer came from Kenwood. Jimmy Lamar had played at Southern. Johnny White, Pat Monahan, Jay Kemey, Tim Martin, Dan Hartman, Dick McCallister, and Pete Parr, all from Loyola, played well for the Hounds of the sixties. Mark Price was from Towson Catholic and Marty Quinn from Calvert Hall. Two stellar Stewarts of the same family matriculated from Loyola High. Another Stewart came from Calvert Hall. These Stewarts markedly impacted the team.

At his first practice, Jim Kelly just started knocking people down. It was like dropping the little figures in the Pac- Man game. Batman Wenzel told Jim that he appreciated his enthusiasm, but hitting was limited to the player with the ball or to anyone within ten yards of a loose ball. Modem safety rules have reduced the area to five yards. This revelation didn't dim his enthusiasm for the game. He quickly was added to the faceoff scrum, where hitting was then an allowed part of the battle. A lot of Kelly-type players emerged over the years.

L

John Stewart was the player of the decade in the sixties and is truly one of the finest players ever to wear the Loyola green. He ended up at Loyola by mere happenstance. He was a star halfback at Loyola High and a good lacrosse player on the new team just formed at Loyola. He was recruited by Otto Graham (of Cleveland Browns fame) to play football at the US Coast Guard Academy. After a grueling summer at the New London Connecticut School and a month into fall football practice, John had had enough. A usually very tough guy, John just didn't like the regimen and hazing which went on non-stop at the Academy. He dropped out and was a late registrant at Loyola College. His presence on the Loyola team that spring was transformative. He scored in bunches. He could run forever. He was ambidextrous. He was captain of his team at the North-South game his senior year. He led the Hounds to winning seasons in his junior and senior years. He scarcely ever came out of a game. When his first midfield unit would come out, Batman would send John down to "rest' on attack.

John won two MSA A conference championships as the longtime coach at Loyola High. He has been one of my best friends over a lifetime and was an usher in my wedding. We bought a beach house together. I wrote multiple scouting reports for him over the years. He would call and say, "Hey Diamond, do you have time to watch St. Paul's (or Gilman or whomever) tomorrow?" Diamond was a nickname I picked up from lacrosse exploits, which I will humbly address directly. John was assistant headmaster at Loyola High for four decades. John and I ran the pro Baltimore Thunder box team for several years. I was the titular head as GM and actually hired John as the head coach. But we shared all decisions, and I fully participated in the coaching. Actually, I frequently suited up as a goalie in practice scrimmages. I'd wobble home, sporting black and blue bruises, and my wife, Kathleen, would say, "I see you played again. My husband is nuts!" But, per Billy Joel, it just may have been a lunatic she was looking for!

L

John Stewart had a long and distinguished tenure as assistant headmaster at Loyola Blakefield. In his role he was the enforcer of campus discipline. He was known as Johnny Law. He knew every student trick. He did a trick of his own when he was the last cut from the Loyola High lacrosse team. The day of the first game, John learned that a player was not getting on the bus due to illness. John grabbed the ill player's uniform and sat in the back of the bus with his helmet on to avoid detection. When Coach Miller inserted him in the game, John scored a goal. The Coach, observing John's prowess and daring, let him stay on the team. John adds a rejoinder: "I stepped in the crease when I scored. Love those referees!"

L

As a footnote to the Wenzel family, Chuck grew up to be a star defenseman at Dulaney High and then at Maryland, as his dad. He looked a lot like dad, as he too wore glasses and tended to be a little chunky. But he moved his big body quickly. His teammates gave him the nickname of "The Dancing Whale." A memorable family: Batman, Honey, and the Dancing Whale! It's part of arcane Loyola Lax history.

Charley and I became very close. I know that John Stewart and I were among his favorites. We were each pall bearers at Charley's funeral a few years ago. John was a favorite because he was a great player, but more importantly, a true leader. He was a three-time All American. At that time, he, Tom Wagner, and Ray Whittelsberger were the only Hounds to hold that distinction. There indeed were a handful of second and third team All Americans as well as some Honorable Mentions in those early years. This honor was somewhat muted by the relatively small number of colleges playing lacrosse. My closeness to Charley was unique. My playing days were brief because of circumstance, economics, and grades. After a freshman season in the sun where I played every minute of every game, I decided I wanted to transfer to the Naval Academy. I had grown up in Annapolis and always wanted to be a midshipman. Also, it was free. It had been a stretch for my Mom and I to handle the Loyola tuition, as modest as it was compared to what it is now. Present tuition, without room and board, is forty-eight thousand dollars per year.

In the fall of my sophomore year I began talking to Navy's coach, Bildy Bilderback. He actually wanted me. He arranged to get me a qualified alternate appointment for athletics, namely, lacrosse. So, it was goodbye to Loyola at the end of fall semester. I would be starting over again at Navy, and I didn't want to waste a year of eligibility. I foolishly neglected making an effort in my classes, assuming I would soon start with a clean slate in Annapolis. Late in May Bildy called with bad news. The football team had taken too many of the available alternate appointments, leaving the lacrosse team with only four. Bildy said he had another goalie he was interested in, and he was not going to pick two goalies. He did say that if I could find a congressman to give me an alternate then he would get me in.

A train trip to Washington the next day took me to the House office building in the Capitol. I knocked on every congressman's door in vain. Those were pre-terrorist days, and security was light. You could roam the hallowed halls unimpeded. Armed Clint Eastwood types with walkie talkies were nowhere to be seen. Plan B was to return to Loyola, where some bridges were burned and had to be repaired. Fr. Aloysuis "Wishbone" Galvin, the Dean of Studies, suggested that I try night school to repair the carnage to my transcript and find employment during the day. He was aware of my barren bank account. Evening school worked well. Working different jobs during the day, I continued this course of study and industry until graduation.

What's this have to do with how Charley and I grew close? I told Charley that I couldn't play as a night student. He invited me to practice with the team whenever I could. So, I spent the next four years as a manager, scout, practice fodder, and volunteer, de jure coach through college and my initial year of law school. I learned to study the game. Furthermore, I was playing club lacrosse with the University Club Collegians, a gathering of some of the finest players and coaches in the land. I absorbed the game of lacrosse like a sponge. Players from the Collegians went on to coaching positions at Navy, Hopkins, Hobart, Maryland, Washington College, Princeton, W & L, and others. Charley was presented with exhaustive scouting reports of upcoming opponents by his twenty-year old assistant. I found jobs where I could leave early to go to practice or scout other teams. Two evenings a week it was practice with the Collegians, while the other nights were evening classes. I still have a cigarette lighter engraved with "1963 National Open Champs," my erstwhile junior year of college.

These were the Kennedy years and Camelot. With the cathartic death of the young president, the world stood still for a while. Everyone knows where they were when the news of his assassination broke over the airwaves of radio and TV. John Stewart and I were headed to his house for lunch. We couldn't get any rock and roll on the car radio. It was all instrumental, depressing, funeral music. We knew something bad had happened. We got to John's house in Hamilton and turned on the TV. Walter Cronkite was somberly announcing the young president's death. The mustachioed, avuncular CBS anchor dabbed his eyes with a handkerchief. Something stirred within me. After a mourning period, I determined that I wanted a career in public service. Formerly, it was all sports. The plan had been to get a master's degree and teach and coach. I would be like some of my University Club teammates who taught and coached. As I said, several of these players went on to coach major programs. Although they played for a rival club team, I especially admired Ed Miller and George Corrigan, who coached at Loyola High while pursuing careers in sales. Eddie later would teach and coach at John Carroll High in Harford County. Now my sports heroes were exchanged for political figures. Law school beckoned.

To be like the Kennedys, you had to have cajillions. Old man Joseph Kennedy made a cajillion by being a bootlegger of booze. My Dad, whom I saw sparingly over the years, probably drank a cajillion beers. He reveled in the Irish love of liquid libation. I had applied to the University of Maryland law school and was placed on the waiting list. With the Loyola diploma in hand and law school admission in limbo, I headed to Ocean City to work as a lifeguard during the day and a bartender at night. I sat on my stand watching foolish tourists flail against the wild surf. Pretty girls paraded by in snug bikinis. In the evenings I was Tom Cruise mixing drinks in Kokomo.

In mid-summer the lifeguard Jeep churned the sand to the north of my stand. With gears and brakes screeching, it approached with the mail. I tore open the envelope containing my rejection from Maryland. Taking off the next day, I drove my Chevy convertible across the Bay Bridge to the admissions desk at the University of Baltimore.

Elated to be accepted quickly, I was now a Baltimore Bee. During my four years of evening law classes, I had day jobs as a title abstractor, a probation officer, and as a law clerk to a judge. My love of lacrosse and Loyola were sidetracked for a while. I did occasionally find time to help John Stewart coach at Loyola High and Charley at the College.

𝕃

John Stewart was off in the army serving in Korea. A brother and cousin profited from John's success at Loyola. Younger brother Henry, a good player out of Calvert Hall, wrangled a rare partial scholarship. Cousin Marty Stewart, a stellar attackman out of Loyola High, also got some financial help to come to Loyola. The legacy of John was a good bargaining chip for these Stewarts. Marty and Henry formed two-thirds of a decent Greyhound attack. Pat Monaghan and Johnny White both were solid midfielders out of Loyola High. Dick McCallister was a tough-as-nails face-off man from Loyola. Dick also wrestled. Tim Martin and Jay Kemey were good defensemen from Loyola High. Bob Lister, who also played basketball, was a solid defenseman from St. Johns in Westminster. McCallister, Monaghan, and Kerney all became Marine Corps officers, who served in Vietnam. Semper Fi. These players and a few other kids who came to Loyola from the local Catholic high schools, most of which had only recently inaugurated lacrosse programs, gave the Hounds some respectable teams in the mid to late sixties. They gave Charley six seasons with at least five wins per year.

Then in 1970 Charley won but one game. Due to mild alum pressure, Charley was gone. He was replaced by a rec council coach who made a living as a physical therapist. Jim Bamhardt was a good guy with suspect coaching credentials. He lasted two seasons with his final year showing one win. Goodbye Jim. In fairness, he was a terrific therapist, with Popeye-like forearms who taught PT at the University of Maryland Medical School, in addition to maintaining a thriving PT practice. But deep tissue massage didn't translate to fast-break defense. Although it did help in treating muscle pulls.

The next hire was Rick Buck with no coaching experience to speak of, but an Ivy League pedigree from Brown. He blessed Loyola with two more years of ineptitude. Rick was another good guy, but Loyola just did not have the players. The surge of high school players had declined. His teams won five and lost twenty-two. Rick wasn't unloaded because Loyola still didn't really care. He departed to spend more time in his family business. In the spring of 1974, Rick needed an assistant coach. I was the cross country coach at Loyola in the fall and the tennis coach in the spring. Rick had asked me to help him myself or help him find someone who wouldn't mind being subjected to the ignominy of a losing program.

I happened to know a young man who was an All American on the 1972 University of Virginia national champion team who wanted to get into coaching. I had become friends with Jay Connor because I worked in his dad's law firm. Jay worked part-time in our office doing real estate appraisals and title searches. He did other odd jobs like house painting and frequently showed up in his painter's coveralls. He must have taken Painting 101 at UVA, the University of southern gentlemen. I recommended Jay to Rick, and Jay spent the season as Rick's assistant. Upon Rick's departure the head coaching job became available. Jay stepped into the breach. He guided the team to another stellar year, marked by some catastrophic losses and a final mark of 3–9. The Hounds had mercifully ceased being subjected to the annual Charles Street Massacre with Hopkins but still had some strong opponents who buried them. Losses to BU and Washington College were by at least twenty points each.

𝕃

Jay was frustrated. He had no tools to entice the better players from Baltimore and Maryland. Lacrosse at Loyola was bereft of rides, except for an occasional John Stewart who ventured onto the campus. John got help when he went to the AD and pleaded his case. Basketball was fully funded. Soccer was close. Baseball was close. Of course, the AD was the baseball coach. Jay enlisted my help. I talked Kevin Robinson, a full -time basketball assistant, into taking over tennis for me. I would be Jay's assistant lacrosse coach. The first order of business was to meet with Fr. Joe Sellinger. I didn't make an appointment but just marched into his office in the late spring of 1975. I was greeted by Mary Joy, Fr. Joe's long-time secretary, and Kelly, his faithful black lab, who rose from his nap on the Oriental rug. Mary Joy asked if I had an appointment. Fr. Joe heard our conversation and bellowed "Come on in, Darrell. What do you need?" As I stepped over Kelly, I announced "It's about the lacrosse team, Father."

To which Fr. Joe queried," Why are they so bad?"

"We have no scholarships." I answered. Fr. Joe expressed surprise at this revelation. He asked if he were to authorize scholarships, "Could we beat Hopkins?" Absolutely!

The next day Fr. Joe asked me to go to lunch at his club, the stuffy Baltimore Country Club in Roland Park. Fr. Joe was probably off shaking down the CEO of some big company for a donation to Loyola. So, he instead sent Vice President Steve McNiemey and Treasurer Joe Yanchik. The end result of our extravagant lunch was the promise of a full NCAA commitment of eleven D-II rides. As a bonus I would get one ride a year for my cross-country team. Not sure whether it helped or not that I, as a social BCC member, signed for the lunch as Joe and Steve kept their hands in their pockets.

Jay and I would parcel the rides out at in halves and quarters to maximize the numbers. I began intensive recruiting, via letters and phone calls, from my law office. I had since left Jay's dad's office and was in my own office on Courtland Avenue in Towson Maryland. My partner was Henry Stewart, John's younger brother. I had three clear routes to gain players. My uncle, Daffy Russell, was the coach at St. Mary's in Annapolis. John Stewart was the coach at Loyola High. A good friend of both Jay and me was Mike Thomas, head coach at Calvert Hall. I endeared myself to Jack Arthur, coach at Curley. We gave many partial rides, and we enticed many others to come to Loyola without aid. We only gave one full scholarship, and that was to Calvert Hall's goalie, who was a first-team All-Metro. Fr. Joe actually helped recruit this young man. Father called me at home one evening and said, "I got you a goalie!" Ironically, this stellar player didn't last much longer than the fall lacrosse scrimmage. He was gone by mid-semester for poor grades. He could play lacrosse, but at Loyola you had to study the strict Jesuit curricula. We banked his full ride.

We turned around Jay's initial 3–9 season to a 7–5 mark in 1976. This was the Hound's first winning season since 1967. Henceforth, until 2003 Loyola suffered only 2 losing seasons, namely, Jay's last in 1982 at 6–7 and Dave Cottle's first in 1983 at 5–9. I simply ran out of time at Loyola when I became an assistant public defender in Baltimore County in 1979. But I did continue to help Jay recruit from my law office until he left in 1982. In 1981 Jay took the Hounds to the D-II championship game versus Adelphi, on Long Island.

Jay no longer had me at his side, and the number of recruited players was beginning to dwindle. Graduation of many of our recruits after the 1981 season showed itself in the 6–7 1982 record. Jay entreated AD Tom O'Connor to make him full time so he could recruit and make a fuller commitment to the program. AD O'Connor was lukewarm on support of the program. He had also reneged on the cross-country rides. Jay, frustrated, walked out on O'Connor with no intention of coming back. Overlooked by O'Connor was the wonderful job Jay had done for the program. He was a gem and a true player's coach. The full- time position, curiously, was created after Jay resigned. Tom O'Connor did perfunctorily suggest to Jay that he reapply. Jay was engaged to be married, and his sales position was giving him a steady salary. The thirteen-thousand-dollars offered to be a fulltime lacrosse coach just didn't work. So, Jay declined and some weeks later a coach named Dave Cottle was hired. Thus began a new chapter in Loyola lacrosse. From all appearances, the school was starting to care. At least the board of trustees was paying attention. But there should have been a greater effort to retain Jay.

Dave would be stepping into a program which was hoping to exert itself but had a lot of growing to do. The lax team finally had a field to practice on. During my playing time and my first few years with Jay, we often had to wait for the baseball team to finish before we could get onto the field to practice. We sometimes would have to carry the goals down Cold Spring Lane to a public park, we called the lower forty. We didn't have a trainer as such. We had a full-time equipment manager named Wilson Bean. Wilson got to be pretty good at taping. I did too. Wilson would do the laundering of uniforms and towels. After practice or games, Wilson would be besieged for towels. As everyone begged at once for a fresh towel, Wilson would respond, "I ain't but one man." He became known as "One Man Bean." As baseball was eliminated in a Title IX move, Dave Cottle inherited his own field by default. He would also have a trainer, appropriated from Hopkins, namely, Leroy "Brandy" Brandimore. Things were looking up.

L

Wilson Bean had an assistant named Bobby Harmon. Bobby was seen daily on the tractor mowing grass or moving equipment, including goals and the pole vault pit. When he wasn't on the tractor, he would be doing odd jobs while shadow boxing. He professed to all that he was destined to be a champion. He claimed he was undefeated. We constantly pestered him to let us know when he had a fight. Finally, he announced that he was on the card at the Civic Center, now known as the Royal Farms Arena. Several carloads of students headed to the Civic Center. As tickets were cheap, we filled about twenty-five seats on the floor. Bobby's was the first fight. He came out jumping and moving and shadow boxing air. The jabs didn't land. He was knocked out in the first round. He had been undefeated because this was his first fight. It may have been his last!

L

Jay and I have remained close friends over the years. We have kept in touch with many of the young men we recruited and coached. We have yearly reunions at Christmas. We meet at games during the spring season. I have been to weddings of some of our players and was in Ray Schab's wedding. Ray was one of my uncle's boys at St. Mary's. He may have been the best player of the mid to late seventies. I remember calling Henry Ciccarone, the Hopkins head coach in 1977 and also the coach for the South in the upcoming

annual North–South all-star game, and asking Henry to put Ray
on his roster. We hadn't had anyone in the game for years. The call
was in vain as Henry, although a St. Mary's Uncle Daffy product,
was the Hopkins coach, and Hopkins never thought anyone good
could come out of Loyola. This annual North-South all-star game
has since been discontinued because of its conflict with the NCAA
tournaments. In point of fact, John Stewart, Marty Stewart, Pat
Monahan, and Tim Martin, heretofore mentioned solid players
from the mid to late sixties, were the last Loyola players to be
picked for this season ending classic.

As a state judge, I performed the wedding ceremony for Jay and Bon-
nie on a cold winter night about a decade ago. Jay has three sons from
his first marriage, and I have been the confirmation sponsor for two
of them. They are all fine young men, and Jay's oldest boy, Jason, is
a highly successful stock broker and an officer in the Towson Elks, to
which Jay and I belong. Jay was elected to the National Lacrosse Hall
of Fame in 1995. He asked me to make the speech moving his admission. At the downtown Sheridan hotel, I read a few words from Jay's
high school coach, Bill Thomas. I also recollected that when Jay went
to see Fr. Sellinger about becoming Loyola's lacrosse coach, I suggested he get a haircut and trade his painter's garb for a new suit.
Years later, Fr, Sellinger said to me, "Why don't you get a haircut and
wear nice clothes like Jay Connor?"

Dave Cottle had great success at Loyola. In 1984 Loyola made the decision to go D-I in its entire sports program. That meant a tougher schedule for Loyola and upcoming games with all the big-time lacrosse schools Loyola had avoided for years. Soon, Loyola would be playing Navy, Maryland, Hopkins, Virginia, and others. And Loyola would hold its own. They would eventually score wins over all these legendary programs. And the Charles Street Massacre would be reborn and simply be called "The Battle of Charles Street." In 1990 Dave would take his team to the national championship game with Syracuse and the Gait brothers at Rutgers University in New Jersey. Syracuse won the game 21–9 but later the title was stripped because of an NCAA violation incurred by the Orangemen. But the NCAA did not cede the title to Loyola. Had the losing team been Maryland, Duke, Virginia or, heaven forbid, the great Johns Hopkins, it would have happened. Loyola is still a small player among big schools, but the Hounds continue to be the little engine that could. Their national championship would come, in the Lord's good time.

But every bit as pivotal as the two NCAA championship appearances was the 1981 D-II championship game at Adelphi. It was the first statement that Loyola could play on a big stage and that the school really cared. It was catching up to basketball on campus. It was right there with the very popular soccer team, the 1975 D-II national champ. Twenty-five years after the '81 game, the team was recognized at halftime of a Loyola game on campus at Evergreen. Although I was not a part the '81 team, Jay insisted that I step on the field and be recognized with them. He said that I deserved to be there, as I had recruited most of the team. We will talk about these and other players of note in these pages. Their ghosts linger over the new facility called Ridley Athletic Complex, a sixty-eight-million-dollar testament.to the arrival of lacrosse at Loyola as their showcase sport. The soccer team would be a co-tenant, but its crowds are usually short of those of lacrosse. The women's soccer and lacrosse teams also share the facility, but their crowds, although enthusiastic, aren't quite the robust crowds of men's lacrosse. Meanwhile the Jesuits were still pursuing excellence in the classroom.

Loyola Chapel: Venue of heavenly supplications for lacrosse success

You can't always get what you want. You can't always
get what you want. But if you try, sometimes, you just
might find, you get what you need.

Mick Jagger and Keith Richards

CHAPTER FOUR:

BOOKENDS OF HOUND LACROSSE

As I transferred my love of sport and lacrosse to politics and law, I had earlier transferred my love of football to lacrosse. It happened on a chilly, early spring afternoon, about a lifetime ago. It occurred on the Loyola College athletic field, which was a far cry from Ridley, with its thousands of stadium seats on two levels and its rich green AstroTurf playing surface. This old field had a few seats, mostly arranged around a baseball diamond, which cut diagonally onto the lacrosse field. Fresh grass was also a rare commodity, especially where the base paths and pitcher's mound intruded defiantly into the lacrosse field.

There was a young man, born in Annapolis, who grew up idolizing Navy gridiron stars and Heisman winners, Joe Bellino and Roger Staubach. He also looked to the Baltimore Colts for heroes, choosing players like Johnny Unitas, Raymond Berry, and Lenny Moore. In a betrayal of family genes, he did not show signs of athletic prowess. He lacked size, speed, and strength. After his parent's divorce, his Mom moved to Baltimore with her son to seek better job opportunities. Her parents had preceded her move to Baltimore and were living in Gardenville, a short walk from St. Anthony's church. Mom and son initially lived in the basement apartment of her parent's home before securing an apartment in the Govans area of north Baltimore. The kid had walked to St. Anthony's to school. Now he walked to St. Mary's in Govans.

The boy saw less of his dad, known as Eggy Russell, because of geography. It was a long Ritchie Highway drive from Annapolis to Baltimore. There were few expressways, as the interstate highway system was in its infancy. But the son knew his dad was a lacrosse and football plyer at St. Johns before World War II and the Great Books program foreclosed the sport at the Annapolis school. He also knew that after the war, his dad and uncle, Daffy Russell, played for the Annapolis Lacrosse Club and a semi-pro football team, called Car Credit, obviously named after its sponsor. Daffy would go on to make a career of coaching at Annapolis High and then at St. Mary's High. He started the lacrosse program at both of these schools and is a member of the National Lacrosse Hall of Fame. Daffy's two sons both excelled in lacrosse and football at Annapolis High. Johnny Russell received a full scholarship to West Virginia University for football. Rusty Russell went to Severn Prep after Annapolis High to hone his athletic skills. Johnny was killed in an auto crash on his way back from WVA during spring break. After a brief flirtation with the B U Bees, where he played defense on the lax team, Rusty opted for the business world and began Rusty Russell Sports, supplying most of the local Anne Arundel County teams with equipment and uniforms. Rumor is that the uniforms weren't always the right color or fit. But Rusty was a likeable guy, with infectious wit, and his business flourished.

Meanwhile, Eggy's son, diminutive and thin, was cut from several teams at Loyola High. He wasn't carrying the Russell athletic legacy very well. He matriculated to City College for his senior year after failing English his junior year at Loyola, then duplicating that feat in summer school. During his senior year, he did play as a standout back-up quarterback for the city 15–17 rec league champion, Govans Optimist football team. He perfected well the art of sitting on the bench and looking good. He would frequently grab his helmet as if he were about to get in the game. He perfected this art in later years while grabbing splinters on the bench for the National Open lacrosse champion University Club. *

Spring would come, and he was enchanted by watching the City College lacrosse team, which rolled to the MSA championship. They beat all the public schools along the way. They bested the private school champ, St. Paul's, for the MSA championship. In those days the private and public champs met for the title. The private schools invariably won. He would sit on the grassy slope bordering the playing field, which was at the foot of what was known as the "Castle on the Hill." He'd watch the City team take apart opponents with pinpoint passing, ballet like dodging, and precision rifle shots on goal. The team featured players who would go on to stardom in college. Ray Altman and Stu "Goose" Harrison played slick attack. Marty Pilsch and Larry Levitt were great middies. The defense was anchored by Dan "Schnoo" Snyder. Donnie Evans was in the goal. The kid determined to master this sport and try out at Loyola College next year, where he had been accepted with a sanitized report card from City.

He started daily throwing the ball against the apartment wall where he and Mom lived in tight quarters. His popularity in the neighborhood dwindled incrementally, as a series of windows exploded from flying, hard, white missiles. The smallish apartment was a far cry from the home where Mom grew up in Annapolis, in a stately white colonial with green shutters, proudly positioned on prestigious Duke of Gloucester Street. It was directly across from St. Mary's church and school. Mom had moved back home with her parents after her separation and divorce from Eggy. The kid would watch his uncle's football games on the field behind the school. Lacrosse had not yet been initiated at St. Mary's. So, football carried the vision of hope. The move to Baltimore ended the dream of one day playing for Uncle Daffy.

He started running and lifting weights. He had experienced a growth spurt, making him almost six feet. He eschewed another fall season of Optimist league football to continue preparation for an attempt to play lacrosse at Loyola College in the spring. As he had taken to a daily run, including sprints up hills, he would try out for midfield. This was an approaching reality, despite the continued ingrained love of football. It was difficult to block out the feel of a leather football slapping a cold palm on a chilly fall afternoon. One advantage of lacrosse over football was he could practice by throwing the ball against the wall without the necessity of finding a partner with whom to play catch. The kid was getting pretty good with his stick work. The scourge of broken windows continued.

The spring of lacrosse arrived. It was a time of pre- campus unrest, pre-Vietnam war, the halcyon early days of the Kennedys and Camelot. The last of dirty white snow had disappeared from the Baltimore landscape. Tryouts had begun. Two days of running and drills had the lax candidate wondering if he would make it. Coach Wenzel subdivided his troops according to position. There was an abundance of middies and a dearth of goalies. He discovered that both of last year's goalies had graduated. There were but two goalie candidates preening for attention. They were each backup goalies in high school, so they knew how to play. He made an executive decision. "Coach, can I switch over to goalie?" Football was being nudged out of the psyche and lacrosse was moving up.

To be a goalie, one needs a certain recklessness and fearlessness. It is the most crucial position on the field. Balls fly headward as cannon shots, which cause most to blink and some to duck. It helps to be loose-limbed and quick, not necessarily fast afoot. The kid was perfectly programmed. He was quick and loose-limbed. He was fearless and didn't blink or duck. To him it was "bring it on." It wasn't surprising that he beat out those other two goalies, who perhaps knew more about the game and certainly had more experience. But the kid was surprised, overwhelmed, and grateful to the Lord. He gave thanks in the quiet of the campus chapel.

The first game was to be played on a raw, crisp, but sunny Saturday. None of the other local Baltimore colleges were playing at home, so Loyola's field, devoid of grandstands, was lined several-deep with hundreds of lacrosse enthusiasts, including a contingent of pretty coeds from neighboring Notre Dame College. And in that crowd was Eggy, who had ventured up the Ritchie Highway. The skinny kid wore number seventeen on his Kelly-green jersey. His baggy gray sweatpants gave slight protection to low hard shots, which would repeatedly bounce of his spindly legs. He did not wear a chest protector because of foolishness. His ensemble included helmet, face mask, gloves, groin cup, cleats, and a newly oiled stick from Bachrach's. He also rejected arm and shoulder pads. He wanted nothing that might inhibit his loosey-goosey movement. He didn't fear the ball or the opponents but only feared failure and letting down his teammates. He stood in the goal in absolute amazement on center stage, filled with the thrill of an exciting sport and its contagious camaraderie. Football had been displaced.

Washington and Lee University is an exclusive private college nested in the foothills of an affluent suburb of Lexington, Virginia. Its history traces back to the American Revolution. They also brought a storied history of lacrosse success, fortified primarily by a pipeline of stellar Baltimore prep stars who had been sent there to excel on the lacrosse field before becoming bankers and barristers. Boys carrying sticks morphed into men with briefcases. Last year they had bested Loyola 15–6. They had a stable of Baltimore stars from Gilman, St. Paul's and the like. Despite a handful of saves from the kid, W & L, predictably, was up 4–1 at the end of the first quarter. Coach "Batman" Wenzel was probably wondering if he had done the right thing by playing this inexperienced kid in the goal. The two backups were ready. With a couple of adjustments and confidence growing, the kid shut them down completely in the second quarter. Halftime score was 4–3. With saves accumulating, the Hounds were up 7-5 with five minutes remaining on the clock. The preppie W & L Generals managed to stick two shots in the back of the net to tie the game 7–7 and send the contest into overtime. Two four-minute overtimes proved meaningless, though the kid made a few more heart-wrenching saves. Sudden death had not yet been adopted as the overtime procedure. The Generals were lucky to escape with a tie. The kid had twenty-four saves in his debut, a Loyola one-game record. The Notre Dame girls cheered. Eggy went for a beer.

The following Monday morning, the third sports page headline of the *Baltimore Sun* newspaper read, "Goalie Russell May Be Diamond in the Rough for Loyola Stickmen." The name Diamond was forever etched onto his persona on the Evergreen campus. Henceforth, he was seldom called by his Christian birth name.

L

Eggy stopped by the small Govans apartment after the game. I had finally become a Russell worthy of the family athletic heritage. Eggy drank another beer to that. Friends still call me Diamond, but few remember the pulsating afternoon when I earned that nickname.

L

This game is the first bookend of my love of Loyola lacrosse and was a turning point in a slow upswing of the sport on campus. Our team finished the season with a record of 3–4–2, nothing spectacular, but adequate. Loyola would slowly get better with the influx of the high school players. The only real blemish that year was the traditional shellacking by the Hopkins Blue Jays. It was a pathetic performance by us, as we were trammeled 20–0. I still have the *Sun* newspaper's photo of me on the ground, having dove for a loose ball outside of the crease while a horde of Hopkins players literally ran over me. I have always respected Johns Hopkins as a wonderful learning institution and a great university. It is the largest employer in Maryland with its hospitals and laboratories as well as the university. Its main hospital in East Baltimore is considered the finest in the world. But despite having many friends who wore the Hopkins blue and gray, it is hard to show love for their program and its stifling aura. As Jay Connor has said repeatedly, "There are Hopkins fans, then there is everyone else!" At the other end of the bookend is the 2012 championship game. And there were pivotal games in between.

L

Brian Schultz was a sophomore on that Loyola team that brought the first D-I championship to Loyola in Lacrosse and first for any D-I sport at Loyola. Brian was like many good players of earlier eras, who ended up on campus as good athletes but grew as lacrosse players. The big difference is that the modem era players are better athletes than early era players. Brian lives in Frederick County and played for Walkersville in high school. He was pretty good, but Walkersville isn't close to being in a league like the MIAA. But Brian played on club teams out of season and kept getting better. He wanted to go to Loyola because he wanted to play lacrosse at Loyola, and his family wanted him to attend a Catholic College. Where he lived, in a suburb of Frederick, the closest Catholic high school was fifty miles away, namely, St. Johns of Westminster. He had a good high school career but not good enough to get much attention from college coaches. But Charley Toomey did like him, and Brian got playing time as a walk-on. He developed a strong left hand and actually was the leftie shooter on the extra-man offense during the championship year. And Charley, in his usual considerate style, managed to get Brian partial aid for his senior year. Brian had finally become a starter on attack for his final year of 2014.

Brian describes the championship game at Gillett Stadium in Foxboro as surreal. The air temperature on the turf was 110 degrees. Loyola had beaten Notre Dame in the semis two days earlier with similar heat and stifling humidity. Brian explained that the team was so dehydrated after the Saturday game with the Irish that IVs were being administered by a doctor in the team hotel. The guys were lining up to get their IV liquid energy from bags looped over clothes hangers. Brian said more important than this restorative elixir was the memory of the loss to Hopkins at the end of the regular season. It was a one-point loss in overtime and the only blemish on the 18–1 season. He said that loss was the most significant motivation for the team all through the playoffs. "We might not have won the championship had we beaten Hopkins. It would have made us over confident. Instead we were hungry and angry." Games with Hopkins mean different things to different generations. And sometimes a loss is more impactful than a win. Incidentally, Brian is still a man on the move. Upon graduation from Loyola he began an internship in the athletic department. He was given ever-increasing responsibilities. He now is an assistant athletic director for development. He keeps us alums involved and open to all Greyhound sports and hopes wallets and purses also remain open.

Brian poignantly recalls looking into the stands at Gillett and seeing a sea of green on championship weekend. "It was just green everywhere. We easily outdrew fans of the great Notre Dame on Saturday, as well as the Duke blues and Maryland reds, the other Saturday semi-final teams. And on Monday, the greens overwhelmed the reds from Maryland." Quint Kessinich, ESPN commentator and former Hopkins star and Baltimore Thunder player, remarked on national TV that the Loyola fans travel better than any college in America. Charley Toomey says the reason for the great student fan support is that "Lacrosse is our football team at Loyola." That and the fact that they are now perennially a winner.

The architect of the Loyola championship was Coach Charley Toomey. Charley was the goalie on the 1990 team that played Syracuse and lost a controversial game. Syracuse played one or more ineligible players and were forced by the NCAA to later forfeit the game they had won on the scoreboard. Loyola still awaits the NCAA to declare them the champions. But Greyhounds do not carry the same weight as Blue Jays in the stuffy boardrooms where decisions are made determining the fate of mankind. Sarcasm rules! But justice would have given Loyola the crown.

Charley grew up in Annapolis at the end of Forest Drive, near the Severn River. He attended Archbishop Spalding initially and transferred to Boys Latin for his final two years of high school. He was a stellar goalie. He recalls a game during his freshman year at Loyola when he did well. My Uncle Daffy of St. Mary's sent Charley a congratulatory note with a five-dollar bill. "Go buy yourself a milkshake, Charley. Great to see an Anne Arundel County boy do good!" Charley's BL play earned Dave Cottle's recruiting nod to come to Loyola. He twice earned All American status. He resides in the Severna Park area of Anne Arundel County with his wife, Sara, and daughters, Emma, Sophie, and Lyla. He lives in a tastefully appointed home with his Boston Whaler beckoning for summer, languishing in the driveway. It will be launched into the Severn after the end of the long lacrosse season, and Charley will pursue rockfish and crabs in deference to championships. This restorative experience is high up on his priorities. I look forward to serving as crew.

After his graduation, I drafted Charley to play for our Baltimore Thunder Pro Lacrosse team. He adopted to the box game quickly, but the starter was a Canadian who had more years to master goalie play in the box. After games our players were always given tickets to get free beers at nearby hotel bars. After a game the boys had congregated at a Weston hotel bar in New Jersey near the Byrne Arena, home venue for the New Jersey Saints. Charley was having a beer when a fan approached him and asked, "Did you see that goalie the Thunder put in late in the game? He sucked." Charley knew that goalie well. Although it was more the booze talking by the fan rather than any lacrosse expertise, Charley began thinking that coaching was the direction he should move in as opposed to playing. However, he did play another season in the indoor league as well as a couple of years of club field lacrosse. Charley has over one hundred career wins at Loyola. In the 2012 championship year he was named D-I Coach of the Year and given an award called the Morris Touchstone Award. Before his fourteen seasons at Loyola as both head and assistant coach, he served as an assistant at Navy for two years. Prior to that he was head coach at the Naval Academy Prep School. The service academy experience taught him the importance of conditioning and imbued in him the style of continual aggressiveness, pioneered by Bildy Bilderback.

𝕃

Needless to say, my debut game was high on my list of memorable and signature games for Hound lacrosse. In 1965 Loyola traveled to Hopkins to continue the one-sided rivalry which had continued unabated since 1939, except for the war years. Loyola had never come close to a win. They lost by an abundance of big scores. There were three shutouts. There were losses of scores like 18–1 16–5, 22–7, 29–3, 18–7, and so on. Clearly these scores merited the infamous name of the contest, "The Charles Street Massacre." Only a dearth of teams geographically accessible, to a team with budget constraints, justified any argument to continue this series. That is, from the cost factor of travel expenses, Hopkins was a bargain as they were one mile away from Evergreen. In 1969 the score was 23–4 and Loyola had enough. Batman asked Lefty Reitz, the long-standing AD, to cease putting Hopkins on the schedule. There were enough teams on the East Coast corridor who more mirrored Loyola's profile of studious, practiced mediocrity. Thus, the series was discontinued until 1993, when the Hounds promptly lost again, to continue the streak. The following year, 1994, the streak ended with a 17–15 Loyola win. But Hopkins still continued their mastery of Loyola although the games were at least competitive. Loyola managed to win in 1998 by a score of 8–6. The Hounds did not win again until 2013. The tide has finally turned, as Loyola has won five of the last six contests against Hopkins. It is ironic that the only loss on Loyola's record in their championship season was that overtime loss to the Jays. There was one game during Batman's tenure where the Hounds actually made a game of it.

It was a drizzly, soggy afternoon in the middle of the week. The game was at Homewood, and the obnoxious Hopkins spirit band was ready to lead the boisterous Jays student section in that stupid refrain of "One, two, three and so on—we want more!" Only this day, their vocal chords were well rested until late in the game. Feisty Loyola was making a game of it going into the fourth quarter. Loyola had a handful of those high school students who had played lacrosse. They had a strong attack, featuring Henry Stewart and cousin Marty Stewart. Gene Miles and Denny Palmer rotated at crease attack. Henry was from Calvert Hall, Marty and Gene were from Loyola, and Denny was from Kenwood and was primarily a soccer player. As a crease attackman, he had a unique skill. For loose balls around the crease, in deference to a stick flick, he would kick the ball goalward. Many opposing defensemen suffered a bruising shin shot from Denny's soccer kicks. He scored several goals over his four years at Loyola by this tactic. Not surprisingly, Dennis was often free on the crease as defenders were wary of his cleats.

Lou Becker, Johnny White, Pete Parr, and Pat Monahan were excellent middies also from Loyola. Marty Stewart and Johnny White both would become Honorable Mention All Americans. They also had Dick McCallister from Loyola, a steady defensive middie who also wrestled. He would become a marine, for which he was well programmed. His cigarette smoking didn't affect his stamina at all. But his teammates were fearful of secondary smoke, and Dick, not surprisingly, always had plenty of room to sit on the bench. Marty Pilachowski, another Loyola Don, was also a steady defensive middie and a ground ball vacuum cleaner. On defense were Timmy Martin, Bob Lister, and Dan Hartman. Dan and Tim were Dons. Bob was from St. Johns in Westminster. In the goal was Harry Bregel, who like Dennis Palmer, hailed from Kenwood High in eastern Baltimore County. Denny's brother, Jack, was a middie also from Kenwood.

Henry Stewart had three goals, and cousin Marty had two. Tim Martin, playing defense, brought a clear the length of the field and slammed the ball into the Hopkins net. The teams were trading goals throughout, and the score was 7–6 early in the last quarter. Hopkins scored three late goals, and the final score was 10–6. Harry Bregel had a great game in the goal for the Hounds. Every participant I talked to about this game remarks that they were amused that Coach Bob Scott of Hopkins was so incensed at the narrowness of the win that he kept his team on the field for a long time after the game. He had them do multiple wind sprints and multiple laps around the track that encircled the field. Several days later, I was present at a Loyola practice, delivering a scouting report to Charley for an upcoming opponent. Charley pulled out a yellow legal paper with a hand-written note. It was from Bob Scott. Charley read the words to the team, sitting in various states of repose on the grass. Scotty was effusive in his praise of Loyola's effort. He was a consummate gentleman and a class guy. Loyola would not come this close to a win over Hopkins for another thirty years.

𝕃

Tony Federico was first-team All- Metro as a goalie for McDonogh. He, like John Stewart, only ended up at Loyola by happenstance. He was heavily recruited and accepted a ride to become a Virginia Cavalier. The gentleman from UVA call themselves "Wahoos" for reasons unknown to the world outside of the Charlottesville campus. This is the school started by Thomas Jefferson and the smugness of their superiority rivals that of Hopkins. Tony was a down to earth, eminently likeable Italian kid who just never felt comfortable at UVA. He dropped out after one semester and never wore the Wahoos' uniform. I had known Tony from social occasions but would come to know him much better very soon. Tony had decided to take courses at Loyola in their evening program as I had. We would study together in the library and go to noon Mass together in the chapel, both praying for a remaking of our transcripts and perhaps a return to the glory days of the lax world.

I never took enough day school courses to be eligible to play again. But Tony finally transferred into the day program in the fall of 1963. Batman salivated at the prospect of having Tony in the goal in the spring of 1964. Tony did not disappoint. The team ended up 6–3–1, with only two losses by large scores, namely to the Washington College Shoremen 15–2, and predictably to the Jays 12–1. Tony had actually beaten out stellar goalie, Harry Bregel, who in the preceding year, garnered Honorable Mention All American status. Batman tried to give Harry playing time but Tony started every game and had a great year, carrying the Hounds to a very solid season. It was the best record since the 1941 season of 5–2. In this year of 1964, only John Stewart was an All American. The Hounds played well in every game, save the two big losses, including the usual massacre on Charles Street. Tony was gone after his excellent year. We each finished our degree requirements in the evening college before heading to law school, Tony to American University and I to the Hivy League of the Baltimore Bees.

Tony and I had many youthful adventures together and remained close friends. As attorneys we each specialized in criminal defense. Two of Tony's younger brothers become Hopkins stars in the seventies. Michael Federico was a three-time All American in the Hopkins goal. Philip Federico had his career cut short by a serious injury. He recovered well enough to become one of Maryland's leading malpractice lawyers. Michael found success in the stock market. He has six children, all of whom played lacrosse. I remember many Sunday afternoons at the Federico household when Mike and Phil would have all the Italian players from Hopkins over for dinner. Mr. Tony Federico, Sr. cooked that wonderful spaghettis sauce from fresh tomatoes all afternoon. The aroma of garlic and tomatoes was intoxicating.

Tony was stricken with a cancerous malady a few years ago. On his deathbed he told Phil that he wanted Diamond to do his eulogy. In the sacristy at the Cathedral of Mary Our Queen, Father DeFusco, the young Italian celebrant, asked Phil who was doing the eulogy. Phil said he was doing one and so was Darrell. Fr. DeFusco said," No, no, just one eulogy." Phil said, "You're up, Diamond." Before a packed Cathedral, with former teammates, many friends, his wife and his six siblings, I did my best. I said that Tony's one year in the sun as Loyola's goalie was as good as any year a Loyola goalie ever had.

𝕃

I took two reprieves from my ongoing disdain for Hopkins. While the Federico siblings Phil and Mike were playing, I frequently would accompany Tony to their games. We traveled to Homewood and to away games in Tony's Corvette convertible, usually with the top down. We once traveled to Princeton and then joined the Hopkins team after the win for an exquisite dinner at a first-class restaurant. Another time we traveled to UVA for a game followed by a team dinner at the Boars Head Inn. Always first-class at the Hop. And the top remained down, rain, wind, or snow. The time would come when Loyola too would be first class. But during my coaching and playing years, it was meal money for fast food.

My son Brendan was very good friends and a teammate for a while with Wells Stanwick. They were in class together at Cathedral and then Boys Latin. Brendan lost playing time due to broken bones from skateboarding and snowboarding. Wells excelled at lacrosse and was a four- year starter on attack for the Jays. I became good friends with his family. I rooted for Wells. The Loyola series was on hold during these years. The Stanwicks have a family of eight, all of whom played lacrosse. On Sundays they would parade their eight kids into Mass at Cathedral while the Russells paraded in their four. The Russells all played lacrosse at one time or another but put down their sticks prematurely and before Dad wanted them to. All the Stanwicks excelled at lacrosse at Hopkins, Georgetown, Boston College, Rutgers, and UVA. Steele Stanwick won the Tewaaraton Award and a national championship at UVA. Sheehan Stanwick Burch is an ESPN announcer. I still see Mom, Dori Stanwick, at early weekday Masses. The Federico and Stanwick families are wonderful lacrosse families. They're up there with the Stewarts. So, I admit it. I like Hopkins sometimes. It's actually envy of the Hopkins program which has motivated Loyola. In recent years Loyola has shamelessly attempted to replicate or improve the Hopkins blueprint.

Loyola used to do a weekend trip of two games on Long Island. We would play Hofstra on Friday afternoon. We would then repair to a cheap motel, after a fast food dinner. Charley always threatened bed checks but never really followed through. Usually the Friday game produced a win and on Saturday, the boys ran like they might be experiencing some malady, such as sleep deprivation. No one admits guilt, but there is evidence that some heavy beer consumption transpired on Friday evenings. There certainly was a lot of frivolity. On the 1964 trip, the guys were given to opening hotel doors and dousing surprised players with water balloons. Innocent enough, but the hotel manager was upset that several mattresses were soaked to the point that rooms couldn't be rented for a few days. AD Lefty Reitz announced that this was the end of two-game, overnight trips. Henceforth, Hofstra and Loyola would alternate home games, facilitated by one-day bus trips. The series with Post was discontinued. The Saturday loss to Post was 13–9 and represented the only other loss suffered by the Hounds this pivotal year, except the losses to the WAC (Washington College) and the Jays. The tie was with Delaware, and John Stewart says that they would have won that game if he hadn't hit the pipe on a late overtime shot.

L

Another adventure occurred on the two- day Long Island visit. John Scoglin, a back- up attackman, was a very serious player and student, unlike some of his teammates. A handful of players decided to pay him a late Friday night visit where he was holed up in his hotel room with a reading lamp and books. He was doggedly studying when there was a knock on the door. John proceeded to open the door. He was suddenly overwhelmed by an envoy of several naked players. After expressing outrage at the nude nuisance, he calmed down and was about to go back to the books. Suddenly there was another knock on the door. John opened it and was greeted by the elfin figure of Batman's eight-year-old son, Chuckie. Fortunately, Chuckie quickly recovered from the sight of a platoon of naked men. He most certainly told Dad, but Batman never brought the subject up. His only concern was that his players would not be hungover.

On a day trip to VMI, the players were impressed by the opulence of the facilities of the military school. All was first-class on the campus and in the locker rooms in the gym. A tall attackman for the Hounds, who will go unnamed, was so enamored by the luxuriant quality of the towels and practice jerseys at VMI that he felt compelled to appropriate a few for keepsakes. Lou Becker was aware of the player's petty theft. Lou surreptitiously removed the travel bag containing the ill-gotten treasure from the perpetrator and hid it under a bus seat. The guilty attackman became frustrated and enraged when he could not locate his bag. He stood and turned to the bus occupants and yelled, "Who has my bag? If there is anything I hate, it's a thief!"

Bolstered by the presence of that plethora of Loyola High talent, the 1966 team compiled a positive record of 7–6. The next three years produced records showing about the same number of wins as losses. Most of the good Loyola High kids were gone by 1970. The record was 1–8, and Charley would also be gone. The early seventies were a wasteland until Jay and I placed our stamp on the program. Not only did we get the scholarships we had long lacked to jumpstart the program, but we attempted to have a year-round policy of keeping after our players. Fall ball, as it began to be called, was starting to appear on college lacrosse campuses. It was a simple concept. Teams would have informal practices and scrimmages for a few select weeks before the cold of winter set in. Unfortunately, we had no field available, as the strong soccer team of Loyola daily commandeered the field. Furthermore, Loyola had become coed with the merger with Mt. St. Agnes in 1972, and they now also had women's field hockey angling to get on the one field. Field hockey would eventually be replaced with women's soccer. But fall ball would be a space issue almost until Ridley Stadium miraculously arose out of a city dump two miles from campus.

Jay and I decided to squeeze into a softball field back behind the new dorms. This was after we had gathered our first recruiting class together in the fall of 1975. We opted for twice a week practices and emphasized conditioning. I was still the cross country coach and took our players for jogs over the course which meandered through both the Notre Dame and Loyola campuses and over neighboring streets. The players hated me for leading them over the rolling hills and around the thick oak trees and between brick and stone buildings. I soon realized that this was just too tortuous for these guys whose runs were usually in sprints. So, I switched the running to easy laps around the reservoir on Cold Spring Lane, followed by sprints on the back field. We used the Navy method of constantly passing the ball while running. On Saturdays we would scrimmage if the main field was available. We had our All Metro goalie from Calvert Hall in one goal and yours truly in the other goal. The Cardinal flash would not be around come springtime, but I would be. Unfortunately, I had no eligibility since I graduated a decade earlier. After a few weeks of fall ball, we gave the kids running and weightlifting schedules to employ until we met again at winter's end. We told them goodbye and to be careful with the one barbell which lay menacingly on the hallway floor outside of the locker room. That was our weight room. Don't let the barbell intimidate you, and don't trip over it!

L

When spring arrived and the troops assembled on Hound field, it wasn't long before we knew we had something. In the preceding four seasons the team had mustered a total of eight wins. We now had a bunch of kids who could catch and throw. We didn't have our prize goalie, but we had John "Oaf' O'Ferrall, who was a back- up at Loyola High, and Mike Boulay, a back- up from Calvert Hall. We had Paul "Pinhead" Stanton, a tough defenseman from Loyola, and Ed Eby, an All Metro defenseman, also a Don from Loyola. There was the speedy David "Jets" Sills from Calvert Hall; Jamie Slafkosky and Ray Schab from St. Mary's of Annapolis; Steve Dempsey and Joe Smith from Loch Raven; Paul Pleviak and Bruce Nolan from Towson High; Eddie Powers and Steve Kauffman from John Carroll; Ron "The Shot" Smith from Poly. And there was Tim Carney from New York. We had spirited practices.

Jay arranged a Saturday scrimmage with Maryland Lacrosse Club. This was a team of post-graduates, most of whom were pretty good players. They were just a step behind Mt. Washington, the premier club team. A controlled two-hour scrimmage yielded a tie score. I asked Joe Harlan, the Maryland Rebels coach, if they were holding back or if they were missing some players. He said that we had faced their best. It was going to be a fun year.

Indeed, we almost matched the total of wins of the preceding four years. The final record was 7–5. All of the losses were closely contested, except for a loss to Towson State, which would go on to win the D-II or college division championship. We would get more good players the following year. In 1977, Gary Hanley would arrive at Loyola from Randallstown High in Baltimore County. Jay was skeptical that someone outside of the County triangle of Towson, Loch Raven, and Dulaney was worth a look. But, Jay and I were usually of similar mind. We doubled down to get Gary to come to Loyola. I knew that this kid would be exceptional. He would go on to set school records for total points, which exceeded three hundred. The record would stand until it was broken in 2018 by Pat Spencer, who is inarguably the greatest player ever from Loyola.

Ray Schab was the player of the seventies and Gary Hanley of the early eighties. Ray was augmented by players like Andrew Smith and John "Hondo" Maas from Loyola, Roy Bands and Alex Gavrelis from Dulaney, John "JK" Kellerman from Cardinal Gibbons, Mike Schmidt and Mark Perry from St. Mary's, Tom Crompton from Parkville, Steve Kauffman from John Carroll, and others, many of whom we have earlier mentioned. The recruits of the late seventies properly belong in the annals of the eighties, particularly the D-II championship game against Adelphi in 1981. That was another pivotal game in the evolution of lacrosse at Evergreen. But there were other landmark games before that championship game.

In that memorable year of 1976, we traveled by bus, as usual, to St. Mary's in southern Maryland. The St. Mary's team was pretty good, having won six games. We came in at 6–4 and had been in every game except Towson, the eventual D-II champ. We had to win this game to assure us of a winning record for the first time in a decade. The last game was to be against the very formidable Baltimore Bees, so a win now was imperative. It was an overcast, damp day, with chilling breezes rolling in from the Patuxent River. We came out very sluggish and quickly found ourselves behind the scrappy team from St. Mary's. Fast forward to five-plus minutes remaining in the contest. We trailed the Seahawks 17–12, and things were as bleak as the weather. Jay was beside himself. When he went into his rants, no one took offense because he was truly loved and respected. Often the players even listened. He turned to me and said, "1 can't believe this. I can't take it anymore!" With that he walked back to the bench, and as he was sitting down shouted to me, "Take over." There wasn't time to have a conference or philosophical discussion or look for a priest for consolation or confession. They were all back at Loyola.

I did call a timeout and beckoned to Jay. He waved me off. I decided to switch things around. I mixed the midfields, leaving our three strongest men together. I wanted Pleviak, Ronnie Smith, and Kauffman on the field until they signaled for help! I wanted Steve Dempsey, Rocky Rhodes, and Bruce Nolan available as the relief group. This was before FOGO and rope units became universal. I decided that Eddie Powers, from the third midfield, would rotate with Pleviak in faceoffs if we scored. And then if Eddie got the ball, get the hell off the field. If we got the faceoff, we were to get the ball to Schabby. He was to work his way around the goal. He could shoot or feed. Crompton was to pick and roll off the crease. Kauf would pick up top on the midfield. Very simple. We needed picks and execution and the ball. We got the faceoffs. Pleviak was scooping the ball and heading toward the goal. Eddie was getting the faceoffs and running off and was replaced by Plevs. We got the ball to Ray. We scored eight goals and walked off the field with a 20–18 win.

On the ride back on the bus, game balls were awarded to Jets Sills, Eddie Powers, Ray Schab, and me. It was a wild and raucous ride back. Tom Crompton was so enthusiastic with the win that he had to be restrained from bus jacking. Isaiah, the driver, was grateful that we saved his life because Tom was crazy now and then. He was even worse when we lost. His famous line was, "Just get me the ball!" He frequently responded with multiple-goal games.

This win cemented the boys together for the remainder of the season and for many seasons and years thereafter.

L

Steve Kauffman had some classic expressions. He is now a very articulate business lawyer and CPA. His facility of expression began as a member of the Ten Hounds. At an evening game at Happy Valley at Penn State, we had dug ourselves into another deep hole. We trailed by seven goals at halftime. Jay was still composed but was ripping off a rah-rah speech at halftime. He hoarsely preached, "What we need is every faceoff. What we need is every ground ball. What we need is every clear." From the back of the locker room, where we had gathered in the bowels of the stadium, came a retort which echoed off the walls as Kauf bellowed, "What we need is a friggin miracle!" The laughter also bounced off the walls. We, in turn, bounced out to the field and promptly were bounced by the Nittany Lions 17–12. But the wins were soon to come.

Early D-I Recruits: Learning that the ref's word is unassailable.

"Sports teaches everyone who is a part of it to be proud and unbending in defeat, yet humble in victory...it teaches the dominance of courage over timidity."

Vince Lombardi

CHAPTER FIVE:

BEGINNING TO SETTLE SCORES

It was and continues to be difficult to get the best player from high-profile schools, particularly from the MIAA. In recruiting we actually went after the number two or three player, knowing number one was going to a program of prominence at a big university, including of course Johns Hopkins. Sometimes we would go after a player who wasn't necessarily a player of robust size, but might be a little smaller. We recruited a lot of players like that, such as Scott Hahn, Mike Schmidt, and Tony Golden to name a few. They all played with big hearts and were positive additions to the improving team. We looked at players outside of the MIAA schools.

There was a young man from Randallstown High in Baltimore County who was putting up some good numbers in the County league, which was considered a step or two or three below the MIAA. There were often very good players in the central part of the county at Dulaney, Towson, Loch Raven, and Hereford. But Randallstown was not on the radar. So, when I told Jay that I was going after Gary Hanley from Randallstown, he was understandably skeptical. I knew

Gary would be a great fit at Loyola. I walked him around our campus and offered him a half-ride, which would correlate to a substantial amount of saved tuition over four years. Duke, singularly among the big schools, also was after Gary. He ultimately chose us. He was my best recruit over the several years I had this responsibility of helping Jay give life to a moribund program.

Jay was also skeptical when I told him about a kid from Catonsville High. But Steve McCloskey became a four-year starter in the goal and anchored the defense. It's doubtful we would have made it to Long Island for the Adelphi championship game without Steve. And he was a first team D-II All American his senior year. He is now a partner in a prestigious law firm in Baltimore and an excellent trial attorney. We run into each other from time to time in the halls of justice.

L

By the end of Gary Hanley's sophomore year, he had shattered all of the career scoring records at Loyola. By the time of his graduation, he had amassed over three hundred total points. That was a record that would stand until broken by superstar and Tewaaraton winner, Pat Spencer, in 2019. Gary says that the players we brought in during his first two years laid a platform that carried the team to the 1981 D-II championship game at Adelphi. There were five thousand fans crammed into the intimate stadium at Garden City, Long Island. Jay was not unaware of the suspect history of the Loyola trips to Long Island a decade earlier. The team arrived on a Friday evening and checked into a comfortable hotel not far from the Adelphi campus. Jay didn't want anyone playing hungover Saturday. So, he bought a few cases of beer and put them in his bathtub and iced them down. He told the boys that beer drinking would be right there at the hotel and it would be with moderation and no one was going to leave the building until the bus ride tomorrow to the stadium.

It was a sober, rested team that entered the field for the most important game in the history of Loyola lacrosse. But inexplicably, the Hounds quickly dug a hole for themselves. After being behind 13-7 at the end of the third quarter, the Hounds huddled. To a man they said it can't end this way. They staged a furious comeback and closed to 15-14. It seemed that Gary was involved in almost every score. Among the fans was a loud section of Loyola students who traveled by busloads. This was the beginning of the student green wave which would eventually make them the best traveled student lacrosse crowd in America. Loyola held their heads high as Adelphi scored two late goals to win 17–14.

L

The 1981 season ended with a good record of 11–5. The team would play one final year in D-II in 1982 but they would face it with a team depleted by the graduation of the core of the team, including Gary and Steve. The record would drop to 6–7 and it would mark the end of the Jay Connor era. But there were other games of significance besides the championship game at Adelphi. The 1980 team may have been stronger than the '81 team. Billy Mahon was playing his second and final year on attack, joining with Gary and Tony Golden. After some phone calls and negotiations, Billy had transferred to Loyola from W & L. He was a big strong guy of six foot five and with a shot like a rifle. His statistics rivaled Gary's. He actually broke Gary's one season scoring record, but the following season Gary regained the mark. Gary says if Billy had been around in 1981, Loyola may have beaten Adelphi. But Gary adds that Ben Hagberg, a transfer from

Anne Arundel Community College, ably took Mahon's spot at attack. The '80 team posted the best record ever at Loyola at 10–2. The only losses were to Penn State by two goals and to UMBC, who would win the D-II title that year. Also graduating after 1980 was two-time All American at defense, David "Jets" Sills. The '81 team boasted four All Americans, namely, Gary, Joe Carrier on defense, David Maynes at midfield, and Steve McCloskey in the goal. They were all first team All Americans in D-II. The heart of this team was graduating, leaving an '82 team bereft of its strength on offense and defense.

L

Watershed wins transpired over the four years that Gary Hanley graced the Hound ten. He singles out three particularly memorable games that put an end to losing streaks of lopsided losses. BU, Washington College and Towson had been winning by big scores for many years.

The Hounds had not beaten the University of Baltimore since 1953. They lost 17-8 and 22-7 in 1975 and '74, respectively. These were typical scores over the years as BU was always near the top of the rankings since the inception of their team in 1949. In '76, with our first recruiting class, we came close at 13–10. The Bees were not on the schedule in 1977 but in '78 they came to Evergreen to play on the natural turf field, marred by many stones, the abutting baseball diamond, and a striking absence of real grass. It was overtime and the score was even at 15-15. Tony Golden, a physically strong but modestly sized attackman from New Jersey, a Jay Connor clone of sorts, muscled his way around the goal with time waning. With not much of an angle he threw a low pass in Gary's direction. Or it may have been a shot. The ball sailed low, and Gary thought it might bounce and hit him as he was standing close to the crease with a defenseman draped over his shoulder. Tony's shot struck a stone, which was protruding out of the ground from inside of the crease. The serendipitous rock gave the invading ball a favorable ricochet, propelling it into the upper right corner of the goal. The 16–15 win had repaid the dozens of huge losses to the Baltimore Bees over the years.

The Hounds had not beaten the Towson Tigers since 1968 when Marty Stewart was leading the offense and was earning All American status as the first Hound to be so honored since cousin John four years earlier. It was a hard fought 5–4 win, and the Hounds would not come close again until the '77 team, our second recruited class, lost 15–12. In 1978 the pummeling re-emerged with a 20–12 dredging. Gary's sophomore year of '79 showed a close loss of 13–12. Towson was curiously absent from the 1980 schedule. In '81, the Tigers came to Loyola and their new AstroTurf field. It was nip and tuck in the late second quarter. Jay had pulled stellar defenseman Eddie Eby because he thought Ed was dogging it. Jay just wanted Eddie to sit a bit. The Tigers scored, and Jay sent Eddie in to play a wing on the faceoff. The rules for faceoffs were less restrictive than today. Most hitting by the wingmen was permissible unless it was unnecessary roughness. Eddie was fuming about his removal. He took off after Towson All American Steve Kopf and crushed him. Kopf lay supine and motionless on the ground for several minutes. Today the hit would be a penalty. Then, it was a clean hit. Kopf did not return to the game, which seriously impacted Towson's midfields and the faceoffs. It was a telling factor in Loyola's 15–9 victory.

Loyola had not beaten Washington College since 1962. That was by a close score of 6–5, wherein John Stewart dominated, having had a hand in five of the goals. Washington had run up some huge scores over the years. Their last encounter was Loyola's biggest defeat in that watershed year of our early recruited class of 1977. The Shoremen spanked us 20–12. The series was renewed, and the WAC was visiting

Loyola on the same day as the Preakness in 1980. The evening prior, Loyola held its prom, and Steve Dempsey, to Jay's dismay, pulled an all-nighter. He entered the locker room with a steaming cup of coffee in his right hand, looking like he needed to find a couch. Steve was as good a soccer player as a lacrosse player. He wasn't a prolific scorer but was very smart and played great defense. He only had one shot, namely, a bounce shot which occasionally eluded the goalie. It was a rainy day, and the Preakness was run on a muddy track, and Loyola and the WAC played on a rain-soaked AstroTurf field full of puddles. Jay was tempted to bench Demps, but Steve protested, saying he was ready and felt great. Jay decided to see how he was doing and yank him if he showed prom fatigue. Steve employed his patented bounce shot. Only it didn't bounce because of the puddles. Rather it just skimmed and skipped its way into the goal as the frustrated BU goalie was playing for the bounce that never came. Steve's three goals were the only time in four years that he scored three goals. They were a big part of the Hound's 17–10 win.

Indeed, the first few recruiting years provided the foundation of players that propelled the Hounds into the championship game of 1981. Some of the other players who contributed were Fric and Frac, the Fortman twins, Matt and Mark. We got them in as cross country rides before the AD pulled the rug on those types of scholarships. Steve Dempsey and Joe Vitrano were members of the '76 D-II soccer championship team, whom we borrowed for lacrosse. Mike Fiocco was a surprise walk on from Westminster who became a MedStar heart doctor. Roy Bands from Dulaney became an orthopedic doctor in Annapolis. Billy Mahon played in '79 and '80. Upon graduation he returned to Loyola for grad school. He had a year of eligibility remaining but just didn't have time to play. Gary says that Billy was spectacular and maintains Billy's unavailability hurt big time in the Adelphi game. Jack Ramey was a solid addition from Curley. David Maynes was a terrific middle from Calvert Hall. He was actually one of those players who wasn't a second-tier recruit but a player whom many schools sought. He wanted to go to a Catholic school with a good lacrosse program. He saw Loyola as a coming team and wanted to be part of it. He was an All-Metro player at Calvert Hall. Gary Hanley was also All- Metro but, not coming out of an MIAA school, slipped under the radar of a lot of big schools. Neil Barthelme was my last recruit. He was a second-team All-Metro out of Calvert Hall. He was a freshman on the '81 team and was a solid four-year starter. He recorded over that period sixty-six assists from the midfield.

Other players of note during Jay's tenure were solid defensemen Gary Rice, Wade Dauses, and Moe Bozel. Mike Goode and Steve Klose, another St. Mary's boy, contributed on midfield. Alex Gavrelis and Michael Mahon helped on attack. These players still remained in 1982 except for Gavrelis. But the remainder of our recruits would soon be gone and a new era would begin.

We used to play Roanoke College, which is deep in the Shenandoah Mountains of Virginia. The series was short lived. The teams played four times from '72 to '75. We never won. The series was discontinued for unclear reasons. Accidental vandalism may have contributed to the cessation. It most likely was never resumed because Roanoke went into D-.III while Loyola went D-I. In the last season of play, I was still the tennis coach at Loyola. The tennis and lacrosse teams traveled together on the bus to play their Roanoke opponents. It seems that one of the rambunctious Loyola players broke a dorm window while playing catch before the game. Loyola's AD at the time was Kevin Kavanagh, who was also the baseball coach, and consequently not too fond of the lacrosse team because of the clash of seasons as well as of a clash of cultures. Kevin demanded to know who broke the window. He said that Roanoke was upset about it. I offered to pay for the window. It may have been the broken glass that shattered the series. It was a long bus drive down into the Shenandoah Valley, and there were many closer geographic opponents within a seventy-five-mile radius of Baltimore. I was not just being generous in offering to pay for the window. I was acting out of conscience formed by Jesuit training. I had broken the window, just as I had broken the apartment windows many years earlier.

Coach Russell was involved in another act of notoriety in the year of 1975. I had been the cross country and tennis coach at Loyola since '73. The Baltimore Orioles were embarking upon a fashion statement with their uniforms. In addition to the standard whites for home games and grays for away, the Birds were going to occasionally wear an orange jersey. The team's colors were orange, black, and white, the botanical colors of the Oriole bird. Bob Brown, the PR director of the Orioles, and Al Harazin, the Assistant GM, had concocted a hair-brain stunt to model the new jersey. They would have an accomplished distance runner retrieve a baseball from the Hall of Fame in Cooperstown, N.Y. and carry it along the road while running daily until reaching Memorial Stadium for Opening Day, all the while wearing the bright orange jersey. They contacted me to see if any of my cross country runners would be interested in performing this feat. There was no way I could jeopardize one of my kids to injury. This was a challenge of at least twenty miles a day for two weeks. Further, it subjected the runner to the danger of cars and trucks, although the course would follow back roads and avoid major highways and expressways. The Oriole GM was Frank Cashen. He was a great guy whom I was fortunate to know personally. I called the O's office and got Frank on the phone. I asked him if Bob and Al were serious. Frank replied that indeed they were and what they really wanted was for me to be the runner.

L

Years later, when I was being considered as the first commissioner of the fledging Major Indoor Lacrosse League (which would become the NLL), Frank Cashen sent a letter to the league owners strongly recommending me for the position. I did get the job. It is seldom mentioned that I was in fact the first commissioner of the professional box league, which still exists in the US and Canada in thirteen cities. Fame, what you get is no tomorrow, sang David Bowie.

L

It was crazy but seemed like a great adventure so I acceded to the request to run this impossible journey. Al and I set aside a weekend to chart the course. We drove over the intended roads and made reservations at hotels along the way. It would amount to a marathon a day; that is, 26 miles a day for 14 days. A total of 364 miles. Cooperstown was in the finger lakes region of upper state New York, a lacrosse hotbed. I would be accompanied by a student of my choosing who would drive the Nissan (at that time called Datsun) bullpen car as he followed and assisted me. I couldn't pick any tennis players or lacrosse players or track runners, as it was their season. I enlisted Basil Maas, the brother of John "Hondo" Maas, a starting lax defenseman.

The trek began on Holy Saturday, and I ran twenty-six miles in the rain. On Easter Sunday I ran forty miles in a snow storm and was attacked by big, barking dogs. I barked back at them. On Monday I logged another thirty miles. On Tuesday I was experiencing soreness in my right heel. As I sat in the Datsun, we called the Oriole office on the car phone (this was pre-cell phone) and told them of my sore foot. They suggested we drive to the Binghamton Hospital in New York and have the foot examined. I explained to the Oriental doctor that I had run over a hundred miles in three days. He looked at my swollen foot and then at me and said in broken English: "You are Crazy! You can no run for six weeks!" Like Achilles, I had been felled by the injury arrow. The Oriole office improvised, and the younger members of the staff took turns moving the ball along until I recovered. Basil jumped in with a few miles too. I limped into Memorial Stadium, with my orange jersey and ball in hand and threw out the first pitch.

My reward was a press pass to Oriole games for the next several years. I digressed to tell this story because the attendant publicity of the stunt inured to Loyola's benefit. The *Baltimore Sun* gave daily progress reports. Evening newscasts remarked "Where is Russell now?" It also endeared me to the Loyola administration, whose attention I would soon need to obtain the indulging of the lacrosse program. Fr. Sellinger always found my exploits and challenges to the administration amusing and was grateful that I had helped unlock the sleeping giant of lacrosse on campus. (I was frequently at odds with the athletic administration on issues of minor sports and women's sports in addition to my vocal championing of lacrosse).

But the lacrosse guys never were fond of the long runs I took them on. Basil Maas entered the Society of Jesus after graduation. Our two weeks of insanity may have driven him there.

L

Fr. Joe only once showed impatience with me. We always had a season-ending sports banquet on campus in the Andrew White Center. They would give us a meal and some awards. We would be served soda, coffee, tea, and water to wash down the mediocre feast. One year, Fr. Joe, using his extensive contacts, commandeered a big hotel downtown for our banquet. Along with the usual liquid refreshments of water, tea, and chocolate milk, yum-yum, Fr. Joe had a few kegs of Schlitz beer shipped in. His brother, Frank Sellinger, was the CEO of Schlitz brewing company. Fr. Joe also delivered the GM of the New York Knicks pro basketball team as a guest speaker. By the time the speaker took the microphone, there was a room full of beer-buzzed jocks. So, nobody paid much attention to the imported lecturer, to Fr. Joe's dismay. There was a constant din of intoxicated conversation. He grabbed me later in the evening and said I was responsible for the disrespect because it appeared to be mostly my lacrosse players ignoring the Dale Carnegie imposter. I said to Fr. Joe, "I didn't know that I was the appointed chaperone. Furthermore Father, that guy was really boring!" The next day on campus, Fr. Joe was walking his black lab, Kelly. He strolled by the field as we prepared for our last game. He approached me and said, "That guy was pretty boring!" And peace returned to Evergreen.

L

Basil's brother, John Hondo Maas, served as my assistant coach in the summer Heroes League. After losing to Dave Cottle's team in the initial year of participation, I was asked to return. The league had six teams, and they were assembled by a draft from the coaches. The list of participants came from those college players who had signed up and paid the entrance fee. It was my intention to get my Morgan players back and supplement them with our Loyola players. So, we got many of our recruits on the team but not as many Morgan Bears. A host of Bears had graduated and moved on. Chip Silverman had left to be the State Drug Czar, and Morgan was on the decline. There was a kid named Jamie Forbes who was on the list. He was a goalie from Parkville and was headed to Loyola in the fall. I drafted him not knowing anything about him. This would allow me to play Morgan goalie, Courtney Sevarey, at midfield. Courtney was a great goalie but yearned to leave the constraints of the goal crease and run up and down the field as a midfielder. We started out this way but soon I had to put Courtney back in the goal, as Jamie's skills were too primitive. I don't think Jamie ever played a minute at Loyola. He is now known as James Forbes and is chairman of the Loyola University Maryland Board of Trustees.

The Adelphi trip for the D-II championship was not the first overnight excursion since the folly of trips a decade earlier. Jay and I had arranged three pre-season scrimmages with college and club teams in Florida. This would have been late winter, January 1977. We told the boys that Loyola was not sponsoring this trip and their participation was optional. They would be responsible for carpooling to Florida and paying their own way. This would be a week in the sun during the mini-semester of January, when the Loyola campus was relatively quiet. Many kids on campus routinely headed south during this break. Not surprisingly, almost the entire team showed up at the hotel we had reserved.

There were a couple of Loyola baseball players who came along. They wanted to hit the beach and the dog and pony tracks. They would return to the hotel each evening with wads of bills they had gathered from astute betting. They may have gained their skills from Gambling 101 at Loyola, taught in the Andrew White student lounge! Soon some lacrosse players were giving them small advances to invest on some fast ponies. The lacrosse gamblers realized little or nothing in their returns. Never trust baseball players!

The Florida teams were two colleges in the Ft. Lauderdale area and the Florida Lacrosse Club. At that time there were no Florida NCAA teams. Predictably, we won all three games handily and returned to Baltimore with a feeling of confidence about the upcoming season. It was also a great bonding experience. It may have been a bonding experience for Jay. His girlfriend at the time, Gina, showed up to presumably soak up some Florida rays. I never knew where Jay and Gina disappeared to in the evenings. Nor did I ask. They were probably visiting museums and libraries. When our week's stay sadly ended, I gave Jay the keys to my Mustang so he and Gina could motor north alone and have uninterrupted intellectual conversations. They could discuss the Picassos and Van Goghs recently observed in their cultural wanderings. I bought a plane ticket.

The boys were well behaved for the most part during this trip. So, there was no lecture from the AD about damaged property or players running amok around the Florida Everglades. Any rowdyism was contained and controlled. No one was arrested. Lou Allen may have come close when he made like Spiderman and scaled the wall of a restaurant of sub-par cuisine. And motorists were pulling over as Ron Smith's passengers made siren-like sounds but became mute when the cop car passed. Upon the return of their voices, the boys began making animal sounds. The car became a rolling barnyard. Hardly delinquent activity! Properly reflective of mature college students!

Most of the beer consumed was at the hotel. There may have been a little cannabis smoked, but it was discreet and not widespread. If you walked down the halls of the dorms at Loyola, you might get an occasional whiff of some nefarious smoke. And I think I detected a whiff of the deadly weed on a return bus trip. But Jay and I chose not to be LAPD agents conducting search and seizures. That secondary smoke was fairly strong though, as I recall. But we never had an issue on the lax team. We primarily had All American beer drinkers during a time when the legal age for booze was eighteen.

We had good practices on the fields of Florida International. I mercifully spared the team the long runs and took my homeric jogs alone. We did enough running in our drills, which featured the Navy intensity. It was great fun to leave the field and head to the beach. Only Ray Schab had any surfing skills, learned from spending summers at the ocean. I don't remember anyone else even standing up on their rented boards. Regretfully, this trip was a one-time experience. It provided wonderful esprit but was not repeated until 1990. With the advent of the NCAA tournaments, all teams were now beginning formal practice at the beginning of January. Lacrosse was getting serious now at Evergreen and a trip south would be considered more tomfoolery than practice. Surfer boy Schab now lives in Hawaii. Surf's up!

L

The era of Dave Cottle descended upon Loyola. Dave played very well at a Baltimore City school with a mediocre lacrosse program. But he was for all intents, a lone star at Northern High School, which is located along Northern Parkway in northeast Baltimore City. Salisbury State is located in Salisbury Maryland on the eastern shore. They were a D-III school when Dave enrolled in 1975, and consequently there were no athletic scholarships available. He did get academic aid, but in reality, he wasn't a recruit for any D-I school. But he blossomed as a big-time attackman and scorer for the Sea Gulls. As a freshman he scored over one hundred points. He was also a very smart player who was clearly a field general who directed the offense. He gave us fits when we faced him. Upon his graduation, he stayed at Salisbury as a grad assistant for a year. Then he landed a nice job at the Severn school, an MIAA school situated about ten miles north of Annapolis. He had immediate success and gave Severn a strong presence in the MIAA. He didn't win the title but was close each of the three years he remained with the Little Admirals. That was their earned nickname, as they were once a prep school for the Naval Academy. Now they were perhaps the most prestigious private school in Anne Arundel County.

Jay Connor knew in his heart that 1982 would be his last year, as earlier related. Most of our good recruits had departed. I had ceased my intensive tracking and pursuing players for him and Loyola because of time constraints and knowing that Jay was leaving. In fact, I was running for State's Attorney for Baltimore County and was gone as Jay soon would also be gone. The team ended up 6–7, the first losing season of Jay's tenure since his first year as head coach when he was 3–9. Neal Barthelme, my last recruit at Loyola, Scott Hahn, Dave

Maynes, Mike Mahon, and Steve Klose, for each of whom I had some involvement in their presence on the Ten Hounds, still remained. But the numbers were dwindling. So, the word was out that there would be a vacancy at Loyola, and furthermore, that Loyola would become a fully committed participant in D-I. After three years at Severn, Dave Cottle yearned for the college opportunity. So, he applied after Jay had submitted his resignation.

There had been a perfunctory offer to Jay, but the offer to Dave would be sweetened. As a full-time coach on salary, he would be given recruiting travel expenses. He would also be given access to Loyola's playing field and facilities to conduct summer camps. Not only were these camps instructive, but they were also cash cows to the coaches who ran them. With rent-free facilities, the several-hundred-dollar fees produced a nice profit. There were but token expenses, like salaries for assistants, referee fees, costs of food and drink to hydrate the participants, and insurance costs. Kids brought their own equipment. The school generously provided lacrosse balls. Dave also would now be able to use this forum of his own summer camp as a very convenient recruiting tool. The players would come to him rather than the coach traveling to a myriad of high school games. And Cottle, as well as the soccer and basketball coaches, were given Toyota Avalons in which to travel up and down the East Coast in search of players.

We had left the cupboard bare, and Dave's initial team stumbled to a 5–9 record. He did still have Ben Hagberg and Tom Singleton and the other aforementioned players left from the '82 team, but not much else. With his newly provided resources, which Jay and I never had, it wasn't long before Cottle reloaded. The very next year the Hounds jumped to 10–

4. They had begun a steady climb during the decade which would culminate in the 1990 championship game with Syracuse.

L

John Stewart and I drove to the campus of Rutgers University in Piscataway in northern New Jersey to watch the semi-final game against much-heralded Ivy League champ Yale. In a thrilling game Loyola tied the game late 13–13, sending the contest into overtime. A Chris Colbeck goal won in overtime. My wife Kathleen and I and our two little girls, Eileen and Maureen, made the trip back to Rutgers on Monday, Memorial Day. The Gait brothers were just too much for the Hounds, as Syracuse rolled 21–9. I previously related that the crown was later taken from the Syracuse Orange because of NCAA infractions. Loyola still awaits the delivery of the crown to Evergreen. But instead the NCAA made the decision to just have no champion, an unpopular move. But it's not a surprising move, considering the history of the Lords of Lacrosse. And to its credit, Loyola did not lobby for the trophy.

L

Dave Cottle worked his magic and utilized all the resources he was presented by Loyola. His goal was no less than a rapid rise to the top of D-I NCAA lacrosse. He was bringing in good players all through the eighties. While he was assembling his constantly improving Hounds, I was off in politics and law. I lost a bid to be State's Attorney of Baltimore County in 1982. I was the Democratic nominee but lost to the incumbent Republican State's Attorney, who actually was a good prosecutor who ran a good office. It was tough to get my teeth into issues. But I made a lot of friends. Those contacts helped me immeasurably to become a Judge of the District Court of Maryland. When William Donald Schafer appointed me to the bench in late 1990, I was in private practice with my partner, Henry Stewart. I was also serving as general manager of the Baltimore Thunder of the MILL. Almost the entire Thunder team attended my investiture (swearing in) ceremony in the Towson Court House.

$$L$$

Charles "Buzzy" Sheain contacted me in the early fall of 1986. Buzzy was at Loyola for enough time to have a cup of coffee. That is, he spent a fall semester after transferring from Cornell, and played fall ball with us in 1978. He was a very good goalie from Boys Latin and also was an ice hockey goalie. He had actually played some professional ice hockey. He left Loyola to help his dad in their dry-cleaning business on Loch Raven Boulevard in north Baltimore. After Buzzy's dad passed away, Buzzy sold the business and became a stockbroker. The Baltimore Thunder had been granted a franchise in the new Eagle Box Lacrosse League, which would become the MILL and later the NLL. Buzzy is a gregarious guy with a lot of friends and contacts. He had become the general manager of the newly formed Baltimore Thunder and had hired Bob Griebe as its head coach. Buzz and Bob decided to call on Coach Russell, formerly of Loyola College fame, to see if he wanted to resurrect his coaching career. I was flattered and got permission from Kathleen to jump into this part-time avocation as assistant coach of the Thunder.

My only caveat, which I expressed to Bob and Buzz, was that I knew little or nothing about box lacrosse. They said they were in the same boat and that we'd just figure it out together. I already told you about the opening game, wherein Bob couldn't make it and left me alone in the Baltimore Arena for this first game. We defeated Dave Huntley, of Johns Hopkins fame, and the Philadelphia Wings coach. Chalked that one up for another win for the Hounds over the Jays. Bob Greibe along with Jimmy Darcangelo were the mainstays of the D-II national champion Towson Tigers in 1975. Jimmy was still suiting up and was now on our Thunder team. Bob didn't desert me again for our remaining games, and we rolled to the initial championship.

Another opportunity for a Hound win over the Jays would present itself at season's end. The owners of all four franchises, Chris Fritz and Russ Cline, who were very successful promotors, decided that they needed a commissioner to add some order and professionalism to their league. I don't know who all applied, but I decided to give it a shot. Eventually Dave Huntley and I were flown to the corporate offices of Chris and Russ in Kansas City, Missouri. Going to Kansas City, Kansas City here I come. The opulent offices featured pictures on the walls of some of their famous clients. Madonna seemed to be staring at me. Jon Bon Jovi was pointing his finger at us. Dave and I had separate interviews and flew home together. I felt Dave should get the job, as he had a deeper involvement in lacrosse than I. He was a Canadian who played box lacrosse before coming to Hopkins, where he was an All American on a national championship team. I was surprised when I got the nod. Another win for Loyola over Hopkins! Now I was being called "Commish" rather than Coach or Diamond.

The year as commissioner was hectic. I rented an office in Timonium and hired staff. I couldn't run the league out of my law office, as that would give rise to possible ethical violations of co-mingling. We did manage to write rules that made the game somewhat tamer. There had been a square box drawn outside of the crease, called no man's land. Any offensive player who ventured into this area could be maimed and dismembered and no infraction would be called. Russ and Chris called this their mini-WWF ring. We threw that out quickly before law suits or casualties occurred. But Chris still came into locker rooms before games encouraging the players to start crowd pleasing fights.

We created a rule book, which combined the rules of field lacrosse with those of ice hockey. We hired referees, giving many young officials opportunities only available in field lacrosse after many years of experience and acquired seniority. We negotiated radio and TV deals. We hired new GMs. We bought new turf rugs for our arenas. We negotiated stick and equipment sponsorships. We negotiated marketing deals with arena personnel. We paved the way for expansion.

After a year I feared that my law practice, which Henry Stewart was babysitting, was facing extinction. And Chris and Russ lamented loss of control of their new sport creation. We mutually agreed to return control to Kansas City and rely on a committee of the GMs to jointly advise and consent on league issues. But most of the business issues would revert to KC. I would become the new GM of Baltimore, as Buzzy was moving on. He was going back to being a full-time stock broker with three young kids. Now as GM I would make a concerted effort to get many Loyola Hounds on the Thunder. So, Dave Cottle could stock Loyola while I would stock the Thunder. My first official move was to hire my lifelong friend, John Stewart, as head coach. He protested, as I had when first involved. He said he knew little about box lacrosse. But we were all making it up as we went along. It was a good gig that lasted until Chris and Russ started unloading franchises to local ownership in all of their cities.

This would become another Loyola vs. Hopkins battle. The Thunder was on the market. Ed Hale, the owner of the Baltimore Blast indoor soccer team which shared the Arena with the Thunder, would enlist my help in attempting to buy the franchise. Ed was intrigued by the fact that we outdrew his Blast. Obviously, all the financing would come from Ed and his First Mariner Bank. An offer was made. To our dismay, the KC owners sold the franchise to a Hopkins grad and prominent developer, Dennis Townsend. Chalk up a win for the Jays!

Dennis hired his own staff, which included a new GM and coach. Two years later, attendance had dwindled, and financial losses mounted. Townsend caved and sold the Thunder to a group that eventually put the team in Denver, Colorado. The Colorado Mammoth still plays in Denver in the NLL and averages fifteen thousand per game. There is a time for every purpose under heaven. My time with the Thunder and the MILL was over on earth.

L

Here is what Commissioner Russell wrote, in part, in the MILL game programs, distributed in all of the team's arenas: "Welcome to the MILL The excitement our sport generates fully recaptures the excitement that the Indians experienced. We can almost see the shirtless Indian Braves' sculpted dark forms, gracefully carrying their crosses down the field with the gleam of the sun radiating off their perspiring shoulders, as thousands of villagers cheered them on...." That commissioner certainly had a flair for the dramatic! And let it not be forgotten that he was the first commissioner.

Jenkins Hall: Formerly the library where lacrosse players "rested."

"They got a name for the winners in the world. I want a name when I lose. They call Alabama the Crimson Tide. Call me Deacon Blues."

Steely Dan

CHAPTER SIX:

FINALLY MOVING UP

The new coach's mission was nothing short of an NCAA title. Fr. Sellinger and the board had given him a quiver full of winning arrows to shoot a bullseye for Loyola in the unique Baltimore game, which had been lifted from the Indians. Tom O'Connor, the AD, now had an entire athletic program placed into the highly competitive D-I of the larger US institutions. But the emphasis was to be on soccer, basketball and lacrosse. And Title IX was here to stay so there must be parity for men's and women's teams. And the minor sports would have to make due with a fair but lesser budget. And even for the major sports, the emphasis on recruits would have to favor local players. The three majors for men and women would be given full NCAA commitments for scholarships, but that didn't include room and board. Room and boards would be extended only in selecte instances. But Baltimore and environs continued as a fertile area for the growth of lacrosse players. Soccer and basketball also had a deep reserve of good local players. So, the little school of north Baltimore would be looking primarily in its own back yard. The board had given a quick look at a

possible renewal of the football program, but the costs were too pro-
hibitive. There would be no rah, rah, sis boom bah, and hold that
line! Soccer would do in the fall and in the spring, a strong lax team
would be the showcase replacement for football. For that's the way
it's always been at Hopkins. The Jays have a D-III football team, but
its supporters pale next to the lacrosse followers. At Evergreen, there
was always rampant jealousy of the neighbors down the street. But
the obvious imitation remains the highest form of flattery. Loyola can
boast that the flagstone buildings of Evergreen are superior to the
brick buildings of Homewood!

And who would be that coach who would lead the lacrosse team
to the Promised Land? It would be a young man named Dave Cottle,
just four years removed from his playing days at Salisbury State of
Wicomico County, Maryland.

L

Having fully removed myself from the lacrosse world, and being
ensconced into distance running as an athletic release, I spent my
days as a young lawyer while dabbling in politics. During one of
my long daily runs in the summer of 1973, I literally ran through
the campus of my alma mater, Loyola College. Providentially, I
crossed paths with Ed "Nappy" Doherty, the acting AD and head
basketball coach. Nappy remarked that he had read about me running marathons, and he needed someone to coach the cross country
team in the upcoming fall season. I volunteered that I'd be glad to
help, as I ran every day anyway. He asked that I step inside into his
office and sign a contract. I responded that I didn't need to get paid.
Nappy countered, "You have to sign and get paid or they will want
all of us to coach for free!"

I was now the Loyola Greyhounds cross country coach. This was a challenge accepted with vigor. Athletes were found on campus to fill the roster with twelve runners. The course was at Herring Run Park. It needed to be on campus. I borrowed a measuring wheel from Towson's coach, Ned Britt, and marked off a six-mile course on the grounds of Loyola as well as the grounds of adjoining neighbor, Notre Dame College for Women. Nappy asked me if I had gotten permission from Notre Dame to run through their campus. "Of course, Nap." A little fib with fingers crossed! But the good nuns never complained. Their coeds enjoyed watching our runners breezing through their campus in their "brief" ensembles of shorts and t-shirts. We already had a couple of good runners at Loyola, such as Larry Blumenauer and Frank Lanzi from Towson High and Tom Coyle from southern Maryland. We recruited Matt Wilson from Dulaney and Harry Weetenkamp from Mt. St. Joe; Mark and Matt Fortman from Spalding; Steve and Mark Rosasco from John Carroll, and others. We never had a losing record. Every time we ran against Towson, Ned Britt would ask me to return his wheel. Of course, the wheel had long since been returned.

My most controversial contribution to the cross country team was inviting females to participate. I would always ask opposing coaches if they had any objection to the girls running in the meets. No one did as long as the girl's scores didn't count. Kevin Kavanaugh, who had replaced Nappy Doherty as AD, was not happy about my diversity efforts, which included starting a women's club team, as I was acting on my own without going through his office. Otherwise, Kevin was a good guy. Women's cross country became a varsity sport after my departure.

Winter became spring, and Kevin asked me if I would consider coaching the tennis team. I had some experience with tennis, as I had coached Loyola High's tennis team for two years while teaching

Business Law to the seniors two afternoons a week. I was also helping John Stewart with his lacrosse team. (While on Loyola High's campus part time, I was recruited to head the alumni fundraising drive, which included initiating the Thanksgiving Eve bull-roast reunion. I reminded the Dean that I did not have a Loyola diploma. Consequently, Coach Russell was made an honorary member of the class of 1960). So now I was the Loyola College tennis coach. This lasted for two years and two second place Mason-Dixon conference finishes before jumping into lacrosse with Jay Connor.

My mom had remarried and moved in with her husband into his Rodgers Forge row house. I was provided a room there while finishing my studies at Loyola. But into law school I was offered room and board at my Aunt's Guilford mansion. Dr. Mildred Otenasek, Chair of the Political Science and Economics Departments at Notre Dame College for Women, had been married to neurosurgeon Dr. Frank Otenasek. Frank had run off with his secretary, and after the ensuing divorce, Aunt Milly was awarded the huge family home on Northway, located behind the reservoir that flanked the south side of Evergreen. I occupied the third floor of the McMansion. Ghosts ran amok around the cavernous rooms and hideaways of the big imposing house. Fr. Joe Sellinger asked Milly if she would consider a few student-athletes as borders, as the dorms were still under construction. We had some memorable borders. There were the Whalen twins, basketballers from New Jersey. Milly's three French poodles would go into spasms at the menacing presence of the Whalens. Carl Maio, a diver from Doylestown Pennsylvania, became a life-long friend. He is now a lawyer in Philadelphia. I would later be Carl's best man in his wedding. When he remarried, I officiated at the ceremony as a Maryland state judge. And there were others who stayed in the apartment over the garage.

Because of the proximity to the Loyola campus, I usually began my day with four laps around the three-quarter-mile path that surrounded the reservoir. Then off to the world of law and politics. I would be back at Loyola in the afternoon with whistle in mouth and clipboard in hand. The evenings were spent on the phone recruiting or writing letters to prospective lacrosse players. Eventually, I purchased my own Rodgers Forge row home and lost the geographic convenience of living a short run from campus. These were wonderful years. Those halcyon days were exceeded only by my marriage to Kathleen and the birth of our four kids.

It was a sad day when I resigned from all duties at the college. Sports had given way to politics and law, as it became impossible to live and thrive in both worlds. I would soon be a candidate for State's Attorney for Baltimore County. Burnout had set in.at Loyola. It had become burdensome to advocate for minor sports, women's sports as well as lacrosse. I loved my players, many of whom have remained life-long friends. AD Tom O'Connor, who succeeded Kavanaugh on the merry go round of ADs, wasn't sorry to see me go. The only person I made an effort to say goodbye to was Fr. Joe Sellinger. I entered the President's residence, as I did years ago. Mary Joy didn't ask what I wanted but just ushered me into Father's office. It was a tearful goodbye and thank you. "No, thank you, Diamond," said Fr. Joe.

L

Dave Cottle had no distractions in his mission. He had only one sport on which to focus. Unlike Jay and I, he had no other day job. The athletic budget, the diversity of the whole sports program, the necessity for advocacy of his program, were non-issues. He didn't need a course on Jesuit philosophy. He had been given the arrows, and he would start shooting forthwith. He gathered a handful of good players. His first year losing record quickly turned into a winning sophomore season. After the initial 5–9 season, Dave's Greyhounds rattled off eighteen straight winning campaigns, including fourteen straight NCAA appearances, including the 1990 national championship game.

Dave continued to lead Loyola through the nineties. On his watch the annual game with Hopkins was resumed in 1993. The Hounds finally defeated the Jays in 1994 by a score of 17–15. This ended a fifty-year drought. But the streak of massacres actually ended in a memorable, highly publicized fall game in 1989. Fall ball, as it is informally called, had come into vogue. Choice-Visa was a very popular Maryland credit card. It was nationally owned by Citibank. Citibank was eager to spread the local use of the card. Choice had a handful of interns in their local office in Towson, many of whom played lacrosse. One intern was named Brian Kroneberger. The interns conveyed to the boardroom bankers the high appeal of Baltimore lacrosse. Choice consequently made a marketing decision to sponsor a fall tournament wherein they could pass out paper applications for their credit card. More than five thousand fans turned out at the UMBC stadium to watch the well-advertised doubleheader called the Choice Fall Classic. The main attraction was to be a renewal of Loyola vs. Hopkins after a twenty-year hiatus. The other game was UMBC vs. Towson. Fans filled the stands and packed the adjoining grassy hill, primarily to witness the renewal of the "massacre."

The evening before the Saturday contest, Fr. Sellinger visited the Loyola team practice on their Evergreen field. The team huddled to listen to Fr. Joe, with rapt interest. There was no recollection of him ever addressing or even attending a practice. He used impassioned words to express that it had been his intention for a long time to resign as president of Loyola if Loyola ever beat Hopkins. He said that he loved lacrosse and the team. He begged them to send him into retirement. At speech's end, all were in tears, including Fr. Joe.

With five minutes remaining in the game, Loyola trailed the Jays by five goals. Kevin Beach, a freshman out of Mt. St. Joe, had a shot on goal after a dodge. It had been decided that an arc would be drawn sixteen yards outside of the crease and any score from beyond the arc would be two points. (The pros now use this arc). Midfielder Brian Kroneberger stood outside of the arc and yelled at Beach to kick the ball out to him. Beach complied. Kroney caught it, cranked, and scored. The Hounds scored three more goals in the final three minutes and tied the game. The Hounds won in overtime to the rapturous joy of all the long-suffering Loyola alums and fans. I was on the grassy knoll in tears. Mike and Sue Abromaitis were nearby, with handkerchiefs in hand.

That evening, at about ten thirty, Kroney decided to make a call at the President's house on Millbrook Road. My visits were always in daylight. He admittedly had consumed a few beers. His knocking on the door roused Fr. Joe from a deep sleep. Fr. Joe let Brian into the dark and quiet home as he turned on the chandelier lights. He squinted at Brian with his perpetual cross-eyed look and queried the purpose of Brian's nocturnal visit. Kroney answered, "Father, we don't want you to quit!" Fr. Joe replied, "I love lacrosse. I wasn't serious. I'm not quitting. I just wanted you to win. I don't like Hopkins!" Brian adds that the emotion of that game carried over to the semi-finals the following spring against Yale. They were again three goals down with three minutes remaining. They tied Yale and won in overtime.

L

If John Stewart was the player of the sixties, and Ray Schab of the seventies, and Gary Hanley of the early eighties, then Brian Kroneberger was arguably the player of the late eighties. He, like John Stewart, was an accidental Hound. He had been a standout, All-Metro player from Calvert Hall. He accepted an athletic scholarship to Maryland. To Brian, Maryland was just too big and impersonable. After one semester he left and enrolled at Loyola. Dave Cottle did not even know Brian was on campus. As a transfer he was ineligible. There was no hiding in anonymity the following year. From 1987 to 1990 he scored ninety-five goals. He was a senior co-captain. He was a three-time All American. He was the undisputed team leader. He was outspoken and even brash. He had a love-hate relationship with Dave Cottle. But there was mutual respect. When I was running the Baltimore Thunder, Dave advised that I should draft Brian. He was my first choice in 1991 and became a star player for the Thunder. He is a very successful stock broker and is CEO of the Dyer-Kroneberger group. His daily reports are heard on radio on WBAL. He is a living testament to the many success stories of Loyola lacrosse alumni.

L

Brian drew a foul, early in the 1990 season, for holding. It was actually an over-the-head check known as a pencil neck check. According to the severity of the check, it could be holding, cross-checking, or unnecessary roughness. In this case, Brian had put his hand on the back of the UMBC player while doing the pencil neck check. While Brian waited on one knee in the penalty box, Dave walked over and said to him, "If you ever use that check again, you'll be benched." Brian just stared at Dave, who then said, "Answer me or you'll be off the team." Brian responded with a curt, "Yes, Coach." It was the semi-final game with Yale at Rutgers, there was less than a minute remaining, and Loyola trailed by a goal. Star Yale middie Jonathon Reese, who would later play professional football, was bringing the ball up the field. Brian had confided to Sean Smith and Chris Colbeck that he intended to pencil neck Reese sometime in the game. The Hounds needed the ball. Brian intercepted Reese short of the midfield line. You guessed it. He hit Reese with the forbidden pencil neck check. The ball popped loose without a penalty. Brian scooped it up and sent it downfield. Seconds later Loyola tied the game on a Jim Blanding goal. Brian came back to the bench and again gave Dave a hard stare. Dave made no response.

In the second overtime, Sean Smith stripped a Yale defenseman of the ball behind the crease. Sean threw it to his best friend on the team, Chris Colbeck, who put it in the goal for the win. Chris was one of the three co-captains of this charmed '90 team. The other two captains were Brian and Charley Toomey. Sean, Chris, and Brian all played together at Calvert Hall. Now it was time to face Syracuse and Gary and Paul Gait on Memorial Day for the national championship. This Syracuse opponent was being hailed as one of the greatest teams of all time. Loyola made a game of it for the first half before succumbing to a team with multiple All Americans, 21–9. But more drama than the game itself unfolded during warm-ups.

On the intervening Sunday, between Saturday's semis and the final on Monday, a press conference was held. Charley Toomey and Brian and Coach Cottle represented Loyola. Syracuse was represented by Matty Paylin, Jim Egan, and Coach Roy Simmons. Matty Paylin said to the assembled press that he was told he could not return home unless he brought back the championship trophy. Brian interjected, "You can stay at our family condo in Ocean City when you lose." Laughter erupted all around. Brian noted that even Cottle laughed. Pre-game Memorial Day Monday, Loyola was warming up. Suddenly, the Syracuse team, clad in bright orange, came bursting out of the tunnel like an explosion of orange fire and began an animated lap around the field. Jim Egan departed from the orange blaze and headed straight for Brian, who responded with a stiff arm. A melee ensued as both teams started swinging. The bad feelings continued throughout the game as several other scuffles marred the contest.

Two years later Brian was playing a summer tournament in Vail, Colorado. He ran into Jim Egan, who appeared to still have fire in his eyes. Brian approached him: "Jim, I've always wondered why you came after me before the championship game." Egan responded, "I didn't come after you. We got along great at the press conference and I was just running over to you to pat you on the butt and wish you good luck in the game." Brian, overcome with guilt, responded, "Now I'll have to go to confession for my impulsive error in judgment." The new buddies proceeded to down a couple of beers together as Brian provided Jim with stock market tips.

L

Dave Cottle, by any measure, was a great coach. Although he had his summer camps, he still beat the pavements very hard to get players. He out-hustled rival coaches. He was unique at the time, as coaches at big programs let the players come to them. Schools like Duke, Carolina, Syracuse and Virginia, all had big football and basketball programs, which were attractions in themselves. Now a lot of coaches are beating the pavement, but when Dave began, he traveled an empty street. He was a stern taskmaster. He ran his players hard. If they won, he would ease up. He had a facility for attracting stellar volunteer assistants. Like Jay Connor, initially Dave had only one paid assistant. He rotated that salary among his volunteers. Over his tenure he had assistants of great repute. He had John Tucker, Has Franklin, Dave Huntley, Dave Allan, Pat Lamon, Greg Manley, Vinny Pfeiffer, and Dave Pietramala, to name a few. Often there were multiple assistants lending their expertise. Now the NCAA allows but one volunteer assistant and two paid assistants.

Dave came up with some great players early on. Pat Lamon, out of Severna Paek High in Anne Arundel County, was one of his first recruits. Pat was one of four brothers, all of whom excelled in lacrosse. Pat was originally recruited by Navy and had attended the Naval Academy Prep School after his graduation from Severna Park. The following year he was supposed to enter the Naval Academy. He instead, at Cottle's behest, enrolled at Loyola. In 1984, Pat scored forty-six goals and had eighteen assists for Loyola. Arguably, Pat became the player of the mid-eighties. He still remains third on the all-time point list with 192. Greg Manley, Dave Sherwood, Rusty Pritzlaff, and Mike Ruland out of St. Mary's, were all mid-eighties All-American offensive players. Wayne McPartland and Jeff Bozel; Gary Beach, defensemen, and Tommy McClelland, goalie, were All Americans from that era. Tom, who was from St. Mary's, was an early draft of mine for the Baltimore Thunder. I lost Pat Lamon to the Philadelphia Wings as they drafted ahead of me. John Carroll was another excellent attackman. Timmy Francis and Chris McGovern were part of a solid defense.

A seminal game of this era occurred in the 1987 season. Loyola traveled to Scott Adams Stadium for a game under the lights at Charlottesville to take on number-two ranked UVA. Behind Rusty Pritzlaff's seven goals, the Hounds thumped them 15–8. Loyola, for the first time, vaulted to a ranking in the top five. They remained a highly ranked team during Dave's entire tenure. As Gary Hanley described the '78 team as being the foundation for the '81 finalist, Brian Kroneberger describes the '87 team as the foundation for the '90 finalist team. Jim Blanding was a first-team All American on that 1990 team. Kroneberger and Charley Toomey were second and third-team All Americans, respectively, in '90. Gary Beach was third-team and Chris Colbeck made honorable mention.

For the first time since Jay and I took the team on a Florida trip in 1976, Dave took the team to Boca Raton, Florida, in the spring of 1990. This time Loyola was paying. They stayed at a high-end Howard Johnson hotel. Dave laid out some basic rules. First, if you're not old enough to drink, don't. If you are old enough, don't drink at the hotel bar. Dave warned that the team would pay with a lot of running if his very simple rules were violated. On the initial evening, Dave was not at the hotel to monitor anyone. Brian thinks he had gone to bet on some ponies. There were also no assistants at the hotel. Brian swears he never heard Dave's warning. Brian entered the hotel bar and was greeted by some pretty girls from 'Ole Miss on spring break who beguiled with their southern accents. (My daughter, Maureen, who went to Sewanee in Tennessee and grad school at Alabama Birmingham, has now assimilated the southern drawl. It is beguiling, but I can't always understand her.) Naturally, Brian started drinking beer with them. Soon, many other Loyola players entered the bar and began hoisting beers. They saw Brian drinking, and as he was captain, it must be all right.

Practice the next day at the St. Andrews field was fearsome, with two hours of concentrated running in the blistering Florida sun. Brian relates that it was personally painful, as he never fancied himself as much of a runner.

A few weeks later, Loyola played North Carolina at the Curley field. There were between four and five thousand fans lining the field. Stands existed on the west side of the field, but the temporary stands of the east side had not yet been purchased from the Naval Academy. Fans completely encircled the field. The intimacy of Curley is dearly missed by many. Ridley is actually a great stadium but with stands on just the west side and the other three sides excluded from the fans, there is a sterility about the atmosphere. In any event, the Carolina game was nip and tuck. In the end, the Hounds prevailed by one goal. Brian is convinced that Dave's harsh riding of the players with endless running made a difference. With that win, the team knew they could run with anyone.

𝕃

If you are a small school and without a big-time football or basketball program, you must excel in small matters to succeed. You must have great goaltending. You must have exceptional faceoff men. Loyola has had a plethora of good goalies. Vinny Pfieffer, Tom McClelland, Tim McGeeney, Don McDuffy, Jim Brown, and Charley Toomey from the eighties and nineties, were great. Jim Blanding and Mike Ruland were the best offensive players since Hanley and Lamon. Brian belongs in that group too. Brian says that Blanding and Ruland made it so much easier for him and Kevin Beach, Chris Colbeck, and Dave Sherwood.

Another defining element of this era was the fact that five long sticks were allowed. So, whenever the ball was lost out of bounds, two more long sticks were sent in to compliment the three long-stick defensemen. Plus, the sixth man was a defensive specialist with a short stick. And if you beat the short stick, a back-up was in your face with a long stick. This was the "stifle Navy rule." Those exciting Navy teams that ran and ran with their four midfield units were gone and replaced by a more boring defensive game. For players like Paul and Gary Gait and Tom Maarchek (also from Syracuse) to excel, speaks volumes of their skills, for they were playing against long sticks. Pursuant to fan complaints, the fifth stick was removed in 1993.

An unseen factor in the construct of the Hound teams, particularly the 1990-finalist team, was that not only was Loyola a small school, but their team in actuality was not fully funded. In the '90 season they beat Virginia, Duke, and Carolina. These are all huge schools with at least twenty-thousand students and D-I football teams. Their lacrosse players were not only on tuition scholarships bur also room and board rides. Loyola in '90 had but four room-and-board rides. So, they were not fully funded. Brian calls his Hounds a "Cast of Clowns." That cast was ranked eleventh in '87, fifth in ' 88, third in '89, and second in '90.

When Brian Kroneberger transferred to Loyola, he was ineligible. He played the succeeding three years. At the end of the third season, he assumed his eligibility was exhausted. Dave Cottle came to Brian and said, "We've taken your case to the NCAA, and they have granted you one more year of eligibility." Given their constant battles, Brian replied, "Are you sure you even want to put up with me for another year." It is doubtful that the '90 season of success would have been possible without Kroney.

L

The Cottle era featured some very good faceoff artists. In the late eighties, and including the '90 finalist team, Steve Vaikness and Tony Pavlik faced off with their respective midfield units. They each won over 50 percent of their draws. Zach Thorton was a stellar middie who controlled the FOs in '94 and '95 and was a third-team All-American. He was also an All-American goalie on the Hounds soccer team. Steve Vaikness returned as a volunteer assistant after his graduation and still remains as the prime Hound FO coach. FOGOs are of a more recent era. Tony, Steve , Zach and Joe Maier in the late nineties all faced off and stayed on the field with their middie units. When Jamie Hanford faced off from '95 through '98, he stayed on the field and went to his post on defense.

L

Paul Cantabene was recruited by Cottle out of Rochester, New York. He played for Irondequoit High School, a name that acknowledges the Native American heritage of this area in upper-state New York. It had become a hotbed for lacrosse, and Coach Cottle was able to entice Paul to come south to Loyola. Paul was a rugged middie who excelled on defense, ground balls, and faceoffs. And he could score. He made second-team All-American in his senior year. He was my first draft choice for the Baltimore Thunder in 1993. He promptly became our MVP in his rookie pro year. He played for several years after I left the Thunder. More importantly, Paul went on to a distinguished coaching career. After tenures as an assistant at Hopkins, Maryland, and Towson, he was hired as the head coach at Stevenson University. In his first nine years with the Mustangs, his team went to eight conference championships, winning twice. He won an NCAA D-III championship. He was the Maryland State College Coach of the Year in 2009, his championship year, as selected by the State College Coaches Association. Paul epitomized the importance of the faceoff as a player. He transferred that to his coaching genius.

His office at Stevenson, where he now is enjoying his fifteenth year, is in the bowels of the Mustang Stadium, on the Owings Mills campus of the school. I was trudging down the catacomb-like hallways with my Cole-Haan loafers echoing the percussion of hard leather on tile. *Clack, clack, clack.* A pretty young lady emerged from a room and said, "Are you lost, Darrel?" It was an old friend, MC McFadden, mother of Tewaaraton winner Caitlyn McFadden. Caitlyn and my daughter, Maureen, went to Notre Dame Prep together. MC is a member of the Stevenson athletic staff.

"I'm looking for Paul Cantabene's office, MC." She led me down the serpentine hall to the very end.

"I found this guy wandering the halls looking for you, Paul." He looked very comfortable in his office, sitting at his Associate Athletic Director's chair. Paul, with a grin, said, "This is the guy who gave me my start in pro ball. Thanks, Coach." He began expressing his fondness for Loyola. MC took off and let us boys talk. (While Caitlynn was starring in lacrosse at NDP, Maureen was captain of the cross country and track teams.)

In 1989 there was a lacrosse camp called Top 205. It was an exclusive camp which filled its roster, primarily by invitation. It was the brain-child of Dave Cottle and was held on the Evergreen field and campus. Dave was assisted by highly successful coaches, Tony Seaman of Towson, and Bill Tierney of Princeton. Paul had been invited to the camp and did quite well. Dave invited him to come back to Loyola for a visit. At that time, he was being recruited by Virginia, North Carolina, Delaware, and Syracuse. They were all schools with twenty-thousand-plus students. "I chose Loyola, and it was a great choice. Had I gone elsewhere, I would not have enjoyed the success I've had in the sport I love." He appreciated the small school atmosphere of Loyola with its small classrooms.

Paul came to Loyola on one of those rare full rides with room and board. He didn't faceoff immediately, as that job was being well tended by Steve Vaikness. But Paul's FO duties increased incrementally each year, until senior year when he handled the draws almost exclusively. Chris Flynn faced off with the second midfield unit, but Paul's unit was usually taking the draw. Paul ran on the first unit for four years. For his freshman year, he ran with Kroney. During his senior year, he ran with Kevin Anderson, an honorable mention All-American. Gary Miller, another All-American, was running with Paul during Paul's second and third years. Gary had a brief stay on our Thunder team. Jim Blanding, also from up-state New York, was first-team All-American in 1990. He was third-team and honorable mention in '91 and '92, respectively. During these years, Paul had a supporting cast of All-American defensemen, Gary Beach and Sean Quinn. Kevin Beach was an honorable mention on attack. Despite this strong assemblage of players, Paul felt that by his senior year, the team was on a downward spiral with a loss of players.

During Paul's freshman year, in addition to Kroney, Gene Ubriaco, from Boys Latin, rounded out the first midfield unit. Early on, Kroney, in feigned seriousness, advised his two running mates that he would always draw the long-stick defender, as he, Kroney, was indeed the veteran. So, it was important that they get open so Kroney could drop the ball off to them. But he further admonished that they should get the ball right back to him. Paul and Gene looked at each other, laughed, and replied "Sure, Brian."

Beaner, as he is called, was effusive about his playing days on the Thunder. His daughter pulls out old tapes of our Thunder games and watches them on rainy days. Among his own favorite memories, he hearkens back to the crucial Yale semi-final of '90. On the bus ride to the game, everyone was bragging and outdoing one another with bravado about how they were going to handle the stud and star, Jon Reese. Chris Colbeck stood up in the aisle and shouted, "Shut up you guys. I'm going to get him!" Reese outweighed Chris by about forty pounds. Midway through the second quarter, there was a loose ball in the corner behind the goal. Reese was attempting to scoop the ball, when suddenly a flash of a player flew at him. It was Chris with a flying check. "He torpedoed him and sent him two feet in the air, and Reese landed on his ass. We all went nuts and were fired up the rest of the game."

Paul recalls Brian's pencil neck check of Reese. Kevin Beach had lost the ball out of bounds. Reese was awarded the ball and was about to bring it upfield. Brian screamed for all of us to get away and that he would handle Reese alone. All the team knew what Brian was about to do except Coach Cottle. Brian threw the check legally. He scooped up the now loose ball and sent it to Jim Blanding, who dipped and ducked and scored with seconds remaining. Then of course, the Hounds prevailed in OT. Cottle never made any comment about the forbidden pencil neck check. Brian had done what was needed. Paul admired Kroney as a good leader. "Kroney had his own style and frequently was banging heads with Cottle. My style was different. I avoided confrontations and just sucked it up. Dave left me alone because I just always hustled and was a good soldier." He adds that Dave was easier to play for than coach with. Dave had strong opinions, and if you differed, be prepared to back it up.

In the succeeding years after the title game, the teams were not quite as strong. The Hounds had a very good defense in '93, as Matt Dwan and Stan Ross stood out and Tim McGeeney was exceptional in the goal. Beaner feels that Matt was great and helped him immensely in his development. "He is one of the all-time great long poles." After several years of periodically showing up as a volunteer assistant, Matt returned as a defensive coach. He still remains as Charley Toomey's defensive coordinator. Like Kroney, Beaner was astounded that so many players came back and helped coach. He remembers Dave Pietramala, dressing to practice with the Hounds. Petro guarded Paul, who thought to himself, "Who is this masked man? He is really good." All the big stars who arrived at a Hounds practice and suited up anonymously wanted to take on Kroney "because he talked so much trash."

Paul has two kids, Lilly and Curry. They are both in school in York, Pennslyvannia, where the Cantabenes reside. It's a forty-five-minute drive for Beaner to get to Stevenson, but well worth it. One of the principle attractions of this area of south Pennsylvania is the quality of the schools. Beaner's son is named after Todd Curry, whom Paul idolized as a player for Syracuse. I was able to trade for Todd from the Philadelphia Wings and consequently reunited Beaner and Todd, two upstate New York boys on the Thunder. In addition to being men's lacrosse coach and Associate AD at Stevenson, he wears the hat of the director of athletic facilities. He remains another living testament to the human success stories of Loyola University lacrosse alums.

𝕃

Try as they might, the Hounds never reached the lofty status of the 1990 team during Cottle's remaining years. They did indeed make the NCAAs every year. The Hounds were eliminated in the first round in 1992, 1996, and 2000. The Hounds made it to the final four in 1998. My two sons and I drove to Rutgers on the Saturday before Memorial Day to see the Hounds square off against Maryland. The Hounds were drubbed 19–8. My sons, Graham and Brendan, were on my Cathedral Tykers (6 to 8 years old) team at that time. Also on the team were Brian Holman's two boys as well as John Tucker's two sons. Marcus Holman and John Tucker, Jr. would become All Americans at North Carolina and Virginia, respectively. The leading scorer of that Tyker team was Graham. Brian Holman is now the head coach at Utah. My assistant coach on that Cathedral team of yore was Brian's wife, Laurie. Coach Russell was an early champion of diversity!

L

During the remaining years of Cottle's tenure, the team could not get past the quarterfinals. The year 2001 was Dave's swan song. He left for an attractive offer extended by the University of Maryland. There he would have all the advantages of a truly big university with a blank check for aid to recruits. And those lacrosse recruits would be dazzled by a campus with big-time football and basketball. In Dave's first year at College Park, Gary Williams took the Terps basketball team to the NCAA national championship. Over succeeding years, Dave was often interviewed at halftime of the well-televised football and basketball games. He was truly now on a bigger stage. Fear the Turtle!

L

Dave's waning years produced a host of great players. Jamie Hanford was a three-time All-American. So too were Mark Frye, Mike Battista, Maat Dwan, and Brendan Fry. Several players were two-time All Americans, namely, Zach Thornton, Gewas Schindler, Todd Viscarrondo, David Metz, Gavin Prout, Mike Stromberg, Mike Sullivan, and Tim Oshea. A host of others grabbed the All-American ring for one outstanding year. There was Bobby Horsey, Tim Goetleman, Tim

Ohara, Jim Brown, Joe Rodrigues, Del Halliday, and Sean Heffernan. These were all Dave's recruits, and he left a roster of strong players for his successor.

Mark Frye was the player of the mid to late nineties. He spearheaded an undefeated regular season in 1999. Unfortunately, they were eliminated by Syracuse in the quarterfinals of the NCAAs. Frye, like Pat Lamon, hailed from Severna Park. He scored a career ninety-three goals and forty-one assists from '96 through '99. As a two-time first-team All American, he went on to an outstanding pro career with the Chesapeake Bayhawks of the MLL and played briefly in the Canadian Football League with the British Columbia Lions.

The four years between coaches Dave Cottle and Charley Toomey were a blip on the upswing heritage of Loyola lacrosse.

Donnelly Science Center:
Rudely planted on the cross-country course.

"I've been thinking about all the places we surfed and danced and all the faces we've missed. Let's get together and do it again."

Brian Wilson

CHAPTER SEVEN:

GETTING BACK ON TRACK

If anyone had a closer view of the ups and downs of Loyola lacrosse at the turn of the century, it was Matt Dwan. His credentials steadily rose from freshman year through his senior year. As a freshman he saw a lot of playing time on extra-man defense. He started on defense as a sophomore and earned Honorable Mention All-American. As a junior, he was a second-team All-American defenseman. By senior year, he became a first-team All-American. The elevator was on its way up after a letdown, subsequent to the 1990 championship game. It would keep climbing towards 2001, when Coach Cottle abruptly moved on. Then the elevator crashed, as losing years ensued during the four-year tenure of Cottle's successor. Coach Bill Dirrigl's last three years of 2003, 2004, and 2005 saw losses of six, eight, and eight games, respectfully—certainly not records meriting NCAA tournament invites. None of Dirrigl's four teams made it to the NCAAs, breaking Cottle's streak of fourteen straight appearances. Bye, bye Bill. His dismissal was an affirmation of a new era, where lacrosse success was important to Loyola.

𝕃

Matt went into medical sales after his graduation in '95. Over the next eight years, he would periodically turn up at practice with the Hounds, as did many other illustrious grads. In 2004, he became a volunteer assistant with Coach Dirrigl. In 2005 he became a full-time assistant. When Charley Toomey moved up from an assistant coach and defensive coordinator to the head coach in 2006, Matt became the defensive coordinator. He is now in his seventeenth year on the coaching staff. He had grown tired and bored with sales and got his wife's approval to pursue his true love of athletics, coaching, and lacrosse. (Matt's wife, Michelle, was a two-time All-American for Loyola's women's lacrosse team. She began a career with Black and Decker after graduation and still remains a high executive with the company based in Towson). He would grow into the job until he became the architect of the national champion's defense of 2012.

Matt wasn't highly recruited coming out of Yorktowne High in Westchester County, New York. He had no D-I offers. His brother, Bill, had offers from Syracuse, Hopkins, and Virginia before choosing Hopkins. Matt was largely unaware of the little school north of Hopkins on Charles Street. He just remembers driving past Loyola on the way to watching his brother play at Hopkins. But that little school was the only college to show an interest in Matt. So, he came to Loyola in the fall of 1991 as an attackman and a middie who excelled on defense. During his freshman year, Matt played on both the offensive and defensive extra-man units for the Hounds. Before season's end he gravitated to just defense. His attack days were done as he showed great promise as a natural defender. He would henceforth use only the long pole.

In those days, camps were relatively few in number. So, college coaches had to go visit prospects. Cottle traveled to New York to watch Matt and Jason Foley play in the state high school championship game. This was in July. Matt got a small enticement to come to Loyola, with classes starting two months hence in September. Foley also became a Hound. Timmy McGeeney was the goalie who played alongside Matt for four years. Like Matt, he wasn't highly recruited, hailing from North County High in Anne Arundel County, Maryland. Also like Matt, he was thrice an All-American. Matt cites Jim Blanding, Kevin Beach, Kevin Anderson, and Paul Cantabene as the offensive stars of his playing days. They were the big four and close behind was Gary Miller, who could really shoot the ball. Sean Quinn was a strong defenseman who played alongside Matt. For Matt's sophomore year, Blanding and Miller had graduated, leaving Beach, Anderson and Cantabene to score almost all of the goals.

Matt laments that his Hounds made the quarterfinals in his last three years but got no further despite good regular seasons. The years of 2002–2006 were a wasteland with no tourney appearances. Coach Toomey finally righted the ship in 2007, when the Hounds returned to the tournament. Matt does not blame Coach Dirrigl for the slide. He feels that "we just didn't get the right players. But Coach Dirrigl hustled and worked real hard recruiting." In 2010 in the playoffs, Loyola lost in four overtimes to Cornell. That was the longest playoff game in NCAA history. In 2015, Coach Toomey experienced his first losing season. Six of the losses were by one goal. The record was 7–8. It gets harder and harder to win because so many D-I teams are investing in their programs. And Loyola continues to play the best teams. The Patriot League has many strong teams, but out of conference, Loyola does not schedule weak teams. Rather, they play Virginia, Duke, Hopkins, Towson, Georgetown, and Rutgers, who will be the out-of-conference opponents for 2020. Loyola continues to not only be among the smallest schools in D-I but the smallest school to ever win the title. The Hounds have four thousand students. Among national title winners, Hopkins has the second-smallest enrollment with six thousand students.

Coach Cottle was clearly upset at halftime in a key home game during the '93 season. Cottle went around the room hurling criticism at each player as they sat in terror on their stools in front of their lockers. These were new metal stools, recently installed in front of each player's personalized locker. Everyone was thinking, *Am I next?* He got to Brendan Fry, an All-American defenseman, who was leaning forward with his shirt bunched up at his waist, giving him the appearance of someone carrying a Natty Boh belly. Cottle said, "Look at you, Fry. You're fat and out of shape and you're supposed to be an All American." Cottle soon got bored at chastising everyone and stormed out of the locker room, with the parting command: "Be ready and on the field in ten minutes." Tommy Welsh, a faceoff man from Calvert Hall, stood up and said, "Brendan you do look like you've put on a few LBs!" Fry retorted: "Welsh, you're way fatter than I." Insults ensued all around, and soon all were laughing, which released the Cottle imposed tension from his feigned histrionics. The boys then gathered themselves up, and went out and beat Syracuse for the first time, particularly avenging the '90 title-game loss. The game went into overtime, with the Hounds getting a hard earned 14–13 win.

Matt recalls that Fr. Sellinger had been calling the Hopkins AD, Bob Scott, for years, begging him to play Loyola once again. The series was finally revived in 1993, as Loyola traveled to Hopkins and lost 16–11. The following year the Jays came to the crowded Evergreen field. Matt recalls fondly, "When we beat Hopkins 17–15, for our first win ever over the Jays, we played in pouring-down rain. The field at the old Evergreen complex had that high school feel, with fans packed all around the perimeter of the field. The drizzly, wet day did not discourage anyone. When the game ended, all the kids stormed the field." Matt remembers Paul Cantabene, who had graduated the year before, running around and tackling his former teammates and reveling in the mud. The cozy feel of the old Greyhound field on campus is gone forever. The old field now is primarily used for intramurals. And the ghosts of yesteryear hover in the midst of drizzly days, as in 1994.

The new facility at Ridley brings multiple benefits to the program. To bring a recruit to a game with five thousand fans attending is certainly an attraction. Regretfully, access is limited at Ridley. There is a pavilion behind the north end where frequently tailgate parties are held for alumni, friends, and paying patrons. All other viewing is from the two-level stands on the west side. Fans are confined to this area and cannot encircle the field or lean on a fence surrounding the field as is done, en masse, at the Hopkins Homewood stadium. Further, Hopkins has grandstands on both north and south sides of their facility, which gives a seating capacity of ten thousand. With the standing crowd encircling the field, attendance can reach twelve thousand. This almost doubles Ridley's capacity. But Hopkins has been at this for over a hundred years. Perhaps someday Loyola will add stands on the east side.

Loyola is way ahead of Hopkins in parking. Not only are there ample lots on the north and east sides of Ridley, but Loyola has an arrangement that allows parking at Children's Hospital, south of Ridley. Hopkins parking lots are a mile away south of their field. And their capacity is limited. Consequently, Hopkins lacrosse fans play havoc with all the local residents who find their streets filled by intruders with their autos. In a student service not provided by Hopkins, Loyola employs about a dozen buses to transport its students from the main campus to the games at Ridley. Just as Father Sellinger fought for the lacrosse program and eventually besting rival Hopkins, Fr. Hap Ridley fought hard with the Board, Ridley stadium neighbors, and city government to build the facility which bears his name. Hopkins wins for stadium seating and fan movement but loses big time to Loyola on the parking issue and student accommodations.

Dave Cottle reminded Matt of his high school coach. He barked a lot but was honest and respected. He made his players better. Matt was conditioned to the stern methods of Coach Cottle. Once Cottle was so mad that he kicked everyone out of their newly refurbished locker room. He made the plyers walk to the dorms to shower and launder their sweaty practice garb. He told the players that they didn't deserve the new locker room. Behind the stern demeanor, Dave was knowledgeable and a good teacher. Dave and Charley Toomey have the same policy of recruiting. They get players that other D-I schools have overlooked or didn't want. Then they develop them. Occasionally, they will recruit a player like Pat Spencer, who clearly was a top high school player. Pat signed to come to Loyola in his junior year at Boys Latin. Pat is an exception. Charley and Matt and offensive coordinator Mark Van Arsdale go to remote parts of the country and continent to find players who will fit the Loyola mold. They have gotten players from Georgia, North Carolina, Florida, California, Oregon, Texas, Canada, and many other areas outside of the traditional hot beds of Maryland and New York.

Loyola is at last fully-funded. Loyola President Fr. Brian Linane has allowed for the full NCAA quota of rides, which is at present, 12.6, with no limit on room and boards. Fr. Linane told me that indulging and financing Loyola lacrosse is worth the huge expense. He says that although it is the most attended sport at Loyola, it is far from being a revenue sport. Loyola has no football team, only a mid-major D-I basketball team and thus, no revenue sports. Schools like Duke, Maryland, Notre Dame, and others can have their entire athletic program funded by its football and basketball teams. It makes Loyola's enduring success as a little school even more remarkable. Loyola recruits players with chips on their shoulders, unwanted by the blue-blood schools. And they play with those chips.

Inside Lacrosse magazine has published a list of the top recruits for the incoming 2020 season. They rank the players from number one to one hundred. In the top fifty, Virginia has five recruits. Duke has seven. Yale has four. Maryland has four. Michigan has three. Notre Dame has six. Hopkins has three. Care to guess how many Loyola has, given their penchant for finding their type of players and developing them? They have zero in the top fifty. They have three in the bottom fifty, ranked at ninety-one, ninety-five, and ninety-seven. And so it goes.

L

There was a pivotable game at Evergreen during Matt's freshman year of 1992. They were playing the defending national champs, North Carolina. It was another packed field at Evergreen. I had my five-year-old daughter, Eileen, in tow. The sun was shining. It was the fourth quarter in a close game. Hounds led 7–5. Matt had but three runs all day, and these were on extra man plays. It was faceoff time after Loyola's seventh goal. Coach said to go in and take the wing. Matt got the ground ball and headed down the field. The Carolina defense was manned by an All-American goalie and two All-American defensemen. Matt split the two defensemen and instead of passing, headed straight to the goal. Shot! Save! He turned and sprinted back down the field and realigned improperly, setting up below the pick rather than on top of it. He compounded his error by hitting the Carolina shooter in the head. He got the foul and Carolina scored, making it 7–6. Matt jogged to the sideline, assuming he had just cost Loyola the game. He was sweating buckets, waiting for Cottle to excoriate him. He figured this could be the end of his Hound career. Dave came over to him and said, "That was one hell of a ground ball you got on the face off." Dave had sensed that this was not the time to rip the freshman's head off. The Hounds hung on for the win, a first over North Carolina.

Matt has deep admiration and respect for Charley Toomey. He feels his personality blends in perfectly with Charley's. Charley is more demonstrative, wearing his emotions on his sleeve. Matt is more reserved. Matt says Charley is terrific as a coach. Charley is very receptive to in game adjustments suggested by his assistants. Charley is described as a great leader of eighteen to twenty-two-year-old kids. Charley gives Matt and Coach Marc Van Arsdale great latitude in recruiting. If Matt or Marc have someone they want, Charley says let's go for it. Charley doesn't need to see the player himself. He trusts the judgment of his assistants. It is a consensus that they seek. And during games, Charley again puts great stock in the opinions of his assistants. At halftime, they will huddle together in the tunnel before entering the locker room with the players. At the halftime of this past year's playoff win over Syracuse, Matt suggested that a short stick middie guard Brendan Curry, (Todd Curry's son), as a defensive middie in deference to a defender with a long pole. The other two defensive middies, one of whom had the long pole, would be ready to slide to help cover Curry. Charley accepted the suggestion, and Curry was effectively throttled and Loyola moved on to the next round.

L

I have arbitrarily created bookend games and placed the heart of this paper between those games. The initial bookend was my game in the goal, when we tied a very strong W & L team. My twenty-four saves got me fleeting fame but a lifetime nickname. I had never seen Loyola College play a lacrosse game prior to that pulsating day against the W & L Generals. I actually don't ever remember seeing any college or club game before my own first game. I had only watched the City College high school team roll through opponents in 1959. There wasn't any particular game of consequence in Loyola annals which transpired prior to the sixties. When Loyola began play in 1938, there was scarcely a ripple of notice in the world of sport. Ironically, that year the world did turn its attention to Baltimore, as a classic race occurred at the Preakness. Horseracing in those days was on the same level as boxing, baseball, and college football. It was a showdown at Pimlico racetrack between two legendary, undefeated stallions named Seabiscuit and War Admiral.

Little did the world or even Baltimore care that Loyola was fielding a team of mostly sophomores who had prevailed upon the AD to give them varsity status. They had banded together the previous year as freshmen playing as a club. They faced mostly high schools in the area. The Evergreen field had been carved out of the John W. Garrett estate, the B & O railroad magnate. Hopkins still holds onto the property north of Evergreen and uses it as a museum, library, and entertainment complex. Loyola would dearly love to acquire this land, but Hopkins is unforgiving in its desire to retain this sliver of real estate. Loyola was able to purchase an easement to the southern edge of the Hopkins property. It is a fifteen-yard-wide stretch that allowed Loyola to construct a passable roadway along the northern edge of their tract. But there will never be a transfer of the main estate.

I once asked Fr. Bill Driscoll, a long tenured Loyola faculty member affectionately known as Uncle Willy, why Hopkins seems to have such enmity toward Loyola. His answer was that we are Catholic and they are not. It began with Henry VIII wanting to marry Ann Boleyn while still married to Catherine of Aragon. When the Pope refused his annulment request, Henry started the Episcopal church. The Baltimore Episcopal Cathedral is catty corner to Homewood Field, just a lacrosse shot away. During the years of the Charles Street Massacre, many were injured by scythe-like swings of the lacrosse sticks, but no one lost his head like St. Thomas More, the Lord Chancellor who defied Henry. More remained unwaveringly Catholic until his execution.

It was difficult to maintain athletic teams during this era, as it was the waning years of the Great Depression. Loyola's football team was a depression casualty as they folded in 1933. The football team was the first team to be called Greyhounds. Loyola would use its spacious field at Evergreen to entertain visiting schools in lacrosse. They weren't going to travel very far because of tight finances. There is no record of what Jack Kelly was paid to coach those initial Loyola laxmen, and it might be he was a volunteer coach. The very first game was a victory over a mediocre Virginia Cavaliers team, 9–4. The *Sun* newspapers gushed over this initial success, writing that Loyola has jumped into lacrosse "with gusto." The gusto continued with wins over "B" teams from Hopkins, Harvard, and Maryland. The following year the schedule was against

144

college varsity "A" teams, and the Hounds did not fare very well. They defeated Virginia again in 1939, but it wasn't until 1987 that they would gain another victory over the Cavaliers. It was a half a century before the Hounds won any games against elite programs such as Maryland, Duke, Navy, Baltimore, and of course, Johns Hopkins. The 1939 Hopkins score was 20–1. The Hounds were defeated by Navy and St. Johns by identical 14–4 scores.

Before the war, the Hounds did okay against teams like Springfield, Western Maryland, West Chester, W & L, and VMI, all of which are now D-III teams. Post-war victories were modest and usually against teams like Swarthmore, Dickinson, Gettysburg, Western Maryland, and similar small institutions which are now D-III. Some years were miserable. The year before my arrival in 1960, the Hounds won but one game. From '55 to '59 they never won more than two games. During the dark ages from post-World War II until the sixties, there were no signature games that are worth memorializing, try as I might to find them. The Hounds continued to play Hopkins, Maryland, Washington College, Baltimore, and Navy because of economics and geographic convenience. And they continued to be pummeled by these teams and some other teams outside of the state of Maryland arc, such as Virginia, Duke, and Hofstra. It is remarkable that in the course of years, Loyola was eventually able to atone for all of those lopsided losses incurred during the dark ages of Loyola lacrosse.

After the first bookend game, there were noteworthy games that are properly part of the historical lore of the program. The valiant effort against Hopkins in 1965, although a close loss, certainly was noteworthy. It was surely the most significant game of the Wenzel era, which spanned seventeen years and had three winning seasons. There were no other games of significance until the 1976 comeback win at St. Mary's of southern Maryland. It was the beginning of the Jay Connor era and cemented the players together, where they have remained ever since. Two years later these same close- knit guys finally atoned for all the losses to U of B with a 16–15 win. In 1980 the boys finally ended years of losses to Washington College of Chestertown, Maryland with a 17–10 win. In 1981 Loyola at last reversed Towson's dominance with a 15–9 victory. And then, in that important year of 1981, Loyola faced Adelphi for the D-II title. A brilliant comeback from a 13–6 deficit, which fell a little short, will remain in the Hound annals. Those boys recently joined together at a reunion at the sky box of Ridley. We were there to watch a scrimmage between the varsity and recent grads. We took a picture of at least ten of us from that group, hoisting the NCAA D-II runner-up trophy. That was the first of many trophies earned by Loyola men's lacrosse.

In the year of 1987, Loyola traveled to Virginia to face the number-two-ranked team under the lights. The Hounds emerged victorious, 15–9, and made their first appearance in the rankings, where they remained throughout the Cottle era. That year they ended up ranked number five. The fall ball game Choice Classic of 1989, while not a regular spring contest, certainly has become legendary. It marked the first win ever over the Jays of Hopkins. The following spring the same team went to the final four. The semi-final win over Yale in overtime remains a classic. The final loss to Syracuse is important for the fact that they had arrived at the championship from the depths of US lacrosse. It had been a quick climb from being a D-II school only seven years earlier.

Two years later, at crowded Evergreen field, the Hounds upset defending national champion North Carolina. The following year, on the same Evergreen field, Loyola atoned for their title loss to Syracuse with a 14–13 overtime win. Cottle's team was undefeated in 1999 and entered the playoffs as the top seed. Regretfully, their old nemesis Syracuse again beat them in the quarterfinals of the playoffs, 17–12. In 2000, traditional foes Hopkins and Syracuse inflicted the only regular season losses on another strong Hound team. Then, in the first round, Notre Dame, whom Loyola had beaten regularly in recent years, knocked out the Hounds, 15–12. In Dave's final year, 2001, the Hounds suffered regular season losses to Hopkins, Syracuse again (who else?), and Notre Dame. The quarterfinals ended in a heart-breaking loss to Princeton, 8–7. Dave then took his broken heart and remarkable successes to College Park, forty miles down the road via US 1.

L

Bill Dirrigl began well enough, compiling a 9–4 mark in his first season as Cottle's successor. That was not good enough for the NCAAs as the Hounds failed to qualify for the first time in fifteen years. The four losses included thumpings by Syracuse, Hopkins, and Georgetown and a one-goal loss to Butler. The following three years showed a continuing decline, with records of 7–6, 4–8, and 5–8. The natives were restless. The AD, the board, and the loyal alums in unison said Dirrigl must go. Enter Charley Toomey, who was hired from in-staff, despite a national search.

Matt Dwan maintains that Dirrigl just didn't recruit the right players. If the selection of All Americans on your roster is an indication of how good your team might be, then Matt is right as rain. During the period 2002 through 2010, there were no first, second or third-team All Americans gracing the Loyola rosters. There was a handful of honorable mentions. Michael Sullivan, Stephen Brundage, Shane Koppens, and Andrew Spack were offensive players, each of whom were twice named honorable mention All Americans. Mike Stromberg was twice named an honorable mention for defense. In 2009 and 2010, P.T. Ricci and Cooper MacDonnell, respectfully, were honorable mention offensive players. Steve Layne was honorable mention for defense, and John Schiavone made it for faceoffs. Finally, in the championship year of 2012, Mike Sawyer and Scott Ratliff made second and third-team All American as an attackmen and long stick, respectively. The selection committee awarded five other Hounds honorable mention status. No one was first team. But the Hounds were first.

L

A retrospective look at some of the Hounds who shone from decade to decade may be a good intro before looking at Charley Toomey's masterful assemblage of a group that went to the top. Bobby McElroy was a three-time All American attackman of the pre-World War II era. Post- World War II, Ray Wittelsberger was thrice All American as a defenseman. Frank Kimmel in the late forties was a three-time honorable mention All-American attackman. In the early fifties, Tom Wagner was twice honorable mention and once second-team as a midfielder. In the mid-fifties, Bill Flattery was twice an honorable mention as a goalie. Bill was my goalie coach during my tenure, however brief, in the Loyola nets. He was a great guy who really showed me the ropes. He taught me to be fearless and to yearn for the ball in my half of the field.

Mickey McFadden was twice honorable mention in the late fifties. He went on to star for the Mt. Washington Wolfpack for many years. He tragically lost an eye while playing for the Mountie team in the Channel 13 Box Summer League. Mickey's injury would never occur today, with the much more protective helmets and visors. The old leather helmets had only a bar protecting the face. The goalie helmets had cross bars. I once had a ball find its way through the bars and firmly plant itself below my eye. I didn't lose sight but briefly lost consciousness. But Batman kept me in the game after giving me a whiff of smelling salts. Do they even make that anymore? Mickey clearly was the player of the fifties. His son is married to MC McFadden, of the present athletic staff of Stevenson. Tewaaraton winner, Caitlynn McFadden, would be Mickey's granddaughter. Both Mickey and Bill are two Irishmen who have joined St. Patrick, where they play lacrosse on heavenly fields.

L

Mt. Washington was one of six teams that played in a box lacrosse arena constructed behind the WJZ TV station. The games were played on Saturday and Sunday afternoons and were telecast on Channel 13. The league lasted for the summers of '63 and '64. Its demise was in part due to the injury suffered by Mickey. The other five teams were from established area field lacrosse club teams, namely, Washington, Baltimore, Maryland, Catonsville-Brooklyn, and the Collegians. The Collegians were an assemblage of recently graduated lacrosse stars. The Collegians won the first championship. They were so dominant that they determined to stay together to play as a field lacrosse club team in the spring. I played in this first summer league venture as a member of the Baltimore team. I joined up with the Collegians in the following spring. We gained a sponsor in the University Club, and we became the University Club Collegians. We went on to win the National Open Championship in the spring. I stayed around and played the following summer for the Collegians in the box. We won that title too, and I got a key ring for my effort, to go along with the cigarette lighter for the Open title. I didn't play goalie on any of these teams but played as a defender on a five man line, who frequently would borrow John Stewart's stick. His wooden stick was perfectly balanced, and it was a magic stick! My scoring production was minimal, but I played adequate defense. Besides Mickey, Ed Miller and I, no other Loyola player was involved in the box league, which disappeared at about the same time as the Edsel automobile.

𝕃

John Stewart was the player of the sixties. Ray Schab of the seventies. Gary Hanley of the early eighties. Pat Lamon of the mid-eighties. Brian Kroneberger of the late eighties. Jim Blanding of the early nineties. Paul Cantabene of the mid-nineties. Mark Frye of the late nineties. With the turn of the century, the dark ages again enveloped the lacrosse program. No dominant players emerged until Charley Toomey once again brought light to the darkness that had descended on Loyola. There is a biblical strain to repeat scenarios of the Hounds history. The book of Genesis reads, "God saw all he made and indeed it was very good.... On the seventh day, God completed the work he had been doing.... God blessed the seventh day and made it holy." Seven is a number which eerily repeats itself in the rise of Loyola Lax.

When Jay Connor assumed the coaching rein, it was 1975. I became his assistant the following year. From Jay's initial year to the D-II title game in 1981, it was seven years. We changed the tenor of the program in biblical proportions. Dark became light. After '81, there were two years of darkness again, with win-loss records of 6–7 and 5–8. Dave Cottle began in 1983 but was hired in late summer, too late for him to impact the program with his own players. His 1984 team was his team, and it posted a 10–4 winning record. There was a steady rise to the D-I title game of 1990. Count the years. It was seven years of labor putting Loyola at the penultimate level of college lacrosse. It was dark again when Charley Toomey became head coach in 2006. In 2012, Charley took the Hounds to the national championship. It was a seven-year journey of dark to brilliant light, which seemed to gleam from above. This is a Jesuit school. Believers see the hand of the Almighty in the miraculous successes of this small school in Baltimore Maryland, USA. AMDG. (Ad Majorem Dei Gloriam— for the greater glory of God).

L

Our ending bookend is quite naturally, the championship game of 2012. On Memorial Day, May 28, 2012, the dreams of those sophomores of 1938, who prevailed upon Loyola to give them varsity status as an official sport of the College, became a reality. The Lacrosse team would win the national championship. No other sport at Loyola has had such an accomplishment at the D-I level. The venue was an NFL stadium in Foxborough, Massachusetts known as Gillett Stadium, home of the Super Bowl champions, the New England Patriots. Pouring into the stands were 30.000 plus fans to watch a game featuring teams from four hundred miles south who in Maryland were only forty miles apart. Despite their proximity to each other, Loyola and Maryland had not played each other for fourteen years. Their last meeting was in 1998, with Maryland winning 19–8. Loyola had three wins against twenty losses to Maryland dating back to 1940.

Classes had ended for the year at Evergreen, leaving the campus quiet like a ghost town. But thousands of Loyola students postponed their summer ventures and filled the Loyola section at Gillett Stadium.

Maryland jumped out to a 3–2 lead early in the second quarter. The green Loyola wave was restless. Their fears soon evaporated as the Hounds scored the next three goals, giving them a 5–3 halftime lead. The Hounds had been having trouble with faceoffs, but midway through the second stanza, the rope unit began to master the rake, pick, and scoop. Despite the lack of initial faceoffs, Loyola was controlling the offensive tempo. The Hound defense forced eight turnovers in the first half, stifling a Terps team that reveled in ball control. Amazingly, Maryland would not score again for the remainder of the contest. Eric Lusby, out of Severna Park High School, another Toomey "find," scored four goals. He scored a record-breaking sixteen goals during the four games of the NCAA tournament. Jack Runkle excelled in the goal, directing a stodgy defense and turning away shots. Mike Sawyer, not from a prestigious MIAA team, but out of a school in North Carolina, was a great compliment to Lusby on attack.

At last, Loyola was the best team in the land. They were the kings of the lacrosse world. *The New York Times*, the leading newspaper of the free world, wrote columns on consecutive days touting the accomplishment of little Loyola. *The Times* wrote the next day: "The win for the top-seeded Greyhounds represents a seismic event in the orderly recent history of the NCAA tournament, dominated in the last two decades by a small circle of programs. Now tiny Loyola, a Jesuit school in northern Baltimore, without a D-I national title in any sport, can add its name to that rarefied list." *The Baltimore Sun* gave Loyola a front-page headline and picture. The headline read simply: "Loyola Takes Title." The story began: "The national lacrosse championship title returned to the state Monday, but it wasn't powerhouse Johns Hopkins, or the much larger University of Maryland, that took top honors. Baltimore's relatively small Loyola University Maryland won the its first national Division I title ever, crushing the Terps 9–3, in an all Maryland final . . . in Foxboro, Mass."

On national TV, Charley Toomey said his players "handled every situation with dignity and class this year." He thanked Fr. Sellinger and Fr. Ridley for their patience, perseverance, and prayers to bring Loyola lacrosse to the top. Charley told me that his teams are the flag for the Jesuit school. The Jesuit values are embodied in his players. The Prayer of St. Ignatius Loyola, which is on the opening page of this book, is posted on the Loyola locker room wall. It ends with these words: "To labor and not to ask for any reward, save that of knowing that I do your will, O Lord." In his heart he knows that the NCAA title was God's will. Charley is a humble person and only wants his boys to carry out the Jesuit values taught at Loyola on the field, in the classroom, and in life.

L

It was a seven-hour bus ride from Foxboro to Evergreen. After the field celebrations, the TV interviews, the photo ops on the field, and the celebratory locker room antics, the boys showered and boarded the bus. Charley had the bus stop at a nearby café where the boys could go in and order sandwiches and subs for the trip. He sternly admonished them not to buy beer or alcoholic beverages. When they climbed back on board and settled in their seats, Charley made a proposal. He explained: "I want everyone to enter into an agreement. You must give me your cell phones, and I will place them in an equipment bag. If anyone holds out, the deal is off. Once I have all your phones, I will ask the driver to stop at a liquor store and we will stock up on beer for the ride home." The repeated clink of phones dropping in the bag was a happy sound. The boys could now celebrate among themselves without phones attached to their ears.

At about 3:00 A.M. the bus pulled into Ridley, where the players had left their cars or where their rides were waiting. They walked out to Ridley field and saw their team picture on the tele-screen with the inscription, "National Champs." The boys approached Charley with a request. They wanted to do one final sprint with the clothes they had on, which was primarily khakis and sport coats. They proceeded to run a 120-yard wind sprint from end to end of the playing field. They then gathered at the center of the field, reached heavenward joining hands, and cheered in unison: "Loyola Hounds, National Champs!" The boys headed to the locker room arm in arm. It was dark, but they had the warmth of the sun within them at night. Fathers Sellinger and Ridley flashed cherubic smiles among the stars of the night.

Goal or perhaps a piper: From John Stewart's magic stick

"We are the champions, my friend. We will keep on fighting until the end. We are the champions. We are the champions. No time for losing, because we are the champions of the world!"

Queen

CHAPTER EIGHT:

HOUND HEAVEN

For Charley Toomey, things are always positive. After winning the national championship, the honors cascaded. He was the unanimous Coach of the Year. He was later named as an assistant coach with Team USA. He will be on the sidelines when the USA plays for the World Cup in 2022 in British Columbia. He was admitted to the Chesapeake chapter of the Lacrosse Hall of Fame. He became the first Loyola member of the NCAA Division-I Men's Lacrosse Committee. This group is responsible for championship locations and administration, rule changes, selection of the men's US national team, and public relations in concert with US Lacrosse. In a sense he became part of the ruling swamp, unique for long-disrespected Loyola. Most importantly, he was able to move his boat to a friend's pier. In winter he raises it four feet above the water via a lift. On the boat is where he still charges his batteries. The trailer remains in the driveway but is more of a monument than a carrier of vessels. Early summer morning excursions, with the sun rising on the water, with coffee mug in one hand and fishing rod in the other, are treasured pleasures. It reminds him of similar trips with his dad. It is important to have these escapes to bring peace to the soul. Charley preaches this to his players.

A family man, he takes great comfort that daughter Emily is a junior at Loyola. Sophia is a freshman at Belmont, a Christian school in Tennessee. Lydia is still at home while attending Severna Park High School as a junior. Wife Sara keeps the household together as Charley puts in twelve-hour days during the season and in the off season is constantly in travel mode recruiting and fulfilling his NCAA duties. His teams have reached the NCAAs seven out of the last eight years. His teams have won the Patriot League title five out of the last six years. He exudes praise for the Patriot League. "It is a great league with many strong teams and all members are great schools with great facilities. How could you have a higher standard than to be in a conference with two of the four service academies, namely, Army and Navy?"

Charley began playing lacrosse as a rec league player in the PAL (Peninsula Athletic League). He had a coach, Jimmy Dollar, from UVA, who asked him to play goalie when the starter broke his arm. Jim told him that he wouldn't have to run sprints as he did as a defenseman. Jim would just shoot on him instead. Charley, like Kroney, never liked running and sprints. He would henceforth, like Teddy Roosevelt, carry a big stick! He could not speak softly, as he had to bark orders to his defense. Learning the ropes in the PAL program, he moved on to Archbishop Spalding, where he immediately became the starting goalie. After two years as Spalding's keeper, Charley made a decision. He wanted to play goalie in college for a D-I school. He might not get the attention of the big schools while playing at Spalding. At that time Spalding, on New Cut Road in Severn Maryland, was a B-conference member of the MIAA. It was and remains a fine Catholic high school with very solid academics. But its lacrosse legacy was limited. Charley wanted to explore transferring to an A-conference power. He contacted Boy's Latin coach, Bobby Shriver. He took a tour of the BL campus on Lake Avenue in Roland Park. It was an attractive landscape of New England-like buildings sitting amidst classic homes and gardens. It was the image of the campus of Welton Academy from *Dead Poets Society*. He enrolled immediately and became BL's starting goalie for the next two years. It was a bonus that Bobby Shriver and Dave Cottle were best of friends. Shrives made sure that Dave got Charley at Loyola.

Coach Cottle said to Charley on a luncheon visit to Evergreen: "You've got room and board and tuition covered. Plus, you get two goalie sticks a year." Charley thought, *Wow. if I don't break any of the sticks, I'll never need to buy another goalie stick.* He was sold and became a Greyhound.

L

On the bus ride back from Rutgers after the 1990 title game with Syracuse, Dave asked Charley to consider returning to Loyola the next year as a volunteer assistant, primarily to coach the goalies, as the goalie coach Tommy McClelland (a Thunder player), was moving on. This was an appealing offer. But Charley was headed to frolic in Australia where he would play some lacrosse and relax "down under." Dave called Charley during his sojourn among the kangaroos and wallabies and repeated his offer. He had been working in Melbourne from July to October, and Dave had called Charley's parents for his phone number. Charley returned and got a job at his grandparent's lumberyard in Elkridge in Howard County. After a busy day in the lumberjack business, he was allowed to leave early and head to Loyola for afternoon practices, where he would be a volunteer assistant. During these busy days, he gave two nights a week and a substantial number of weekends to our Baltimore Thunder team as one of our goalies.

A pivotal year in Charley's coaching resume was 1993. He was hired by the USNA to be the head coach of their NAPS (Naval Academy Prep School). He was sent to Newport, Rhode Island, where he was given Naval training and awarded a commission and a uniform with Ensign bars. His prime assignment was to coach lacrosse. He absorbed the Navy traditions, with heavy emphasis on the Bilderback era. His teams would, in perpetuity, always be well conditioned and run, run, and run, as do all teams of the Navy blue and gold. During this successful year of coaching at Newport, Charley made the decision that his career would be as a lacrosse coach.

𝕷

Dave Cottle was more inclined to take the air out of the ball and work a planned offense. Charley was more run and shoot. Charley ran a fast offense. Dave ran a fast defense. The year before the 2012 championship, Charley had the coaches from Tufts University, a D-III program which was noted for getting off fifty shots per game, visit Loyola. Tufts was coached by Mike Daly, a good friend of Charley. Daly is now the coach at Brown. Charley wanted Loyola to get at least fifty shots per game. The Loyola coaches studied the style of Tufts and incorporated some of it in the 2012 season. They would no longer waste precious time getting the rope unit off the field. If Ratliff and his rope teammates got the ball, they could bring it down the field and facilitate the fast break. They could pick and roll. The practices incorporated more offensive drills for the rope unit. Scott Ratliff scored a lot of goals in this fashion, which helped win a championship, and for Scott, All-American honors. This run-run Navy inbred philosophy, actuated by Tufts, still is mimicked by Hound teams. It, however, was recently compromised by the presence of Pat Spencer. The fast break was still operable, but the prevailing object was to get the ball to Pat. All the offense would run through him. Now that he is gone, the go-go concept will be reborn.

In 1994 Navy brought Charley back from the prep school to be an assistant on the Navy varsity. He remained as the Navy defensive coordinator through 1995. The following season, he left Navy to become head coach at the Severn School on Benfield Road near Annapolis. After three successful years coaching the "Little Admirals," Dave Cottle enticed Charley to return as a paid assistant for the Hounds. He there remained until he became head coach in 2006 and Loyola's downward spiral was halted.

L

Charley is proud of the Loyola tradition and its values imbued in his players. After the annual team retreat at Loyola's retreat facility in western Maryland, some of his players traveled to the inner city of Baltimore to feed the poor. He credits the Jesuits who have been advisors and chaplains to his players. He particularly cites Fr. Jack Dennis and Fr. Tim Brown. The team embraces the true meaning of a Jesuit community. Five months after the Hounds won the NCAA title, twenty-six students were killed in a mass shooting at Sandy Hook Elementary School in Newtown, Connecticut. A year later the entire Hound team traveled to Sandy Hook to give free clinics to the school children who had survived the senseless shooting.

L

A watershed game occurred in 2007 when Loyola traveled via United Airlines to San Diego, California, where they would be part of a doubleheader at San Diego State University. Loyola would face Duke, always a formidable opponent. Mike Graham totally tied up All American Matt Danowski of Duke. Andy Spack and Pat Kennedy scored critical goals with Shane Koppens dishing out assists. The Rabidou brothers hustled all over the field. This was a classic one-goal win, 8–7. It was Charley's second season as head coach at Loyola. The Hounds had lost four years in a row to Duke. He feels that it was a key game in Loyola's history. He actually pulled the starting goalie and put in the second stringer in the second half. He felt the backup was more athletic and would be more effective against Duke's fast breaks. The backup shut down the Blue Devils. Charley was no longer on active Navy duty but was heartened by the presence of thousands of sailors in the stands from the nearby Naval base. Mike Abromaitis and Chris Gunkle traveled with the team and did the play-by-play broadcast back to Baltimore. These days the radio broadcasts have been replaced by TV. Gunks is joined by Dave Cottle as the announcers. So, Dave is back in the Hound family. Charley frequently asks Dave to help at practices. Charley says Dave is a brilliant offensive coach and is happy to have him around again.

Chris and Mike were equipped with primitive broadcasting devices, namely, cell phones. They called the game back to Loyola's campus radio station, which transmitted their voices as best they could. They sounded as if they had head colds. Further compounding their performance was an unforeseen issue. The field press box was inexplicably closed. They reconnoitered to an adjoining campus building and used binoculars to accurately identify players and their numbers. And they added drama by exaggerating the field play, which, due to the distance from the field, was often difficult to follow. Rumor is they were nominated for broadcasting Emmys for their performance.

The broadcasting has come a long way since then, as every game is streamed on live TV or telecast on a cable TV sports network.

𝕃

Charley reminisces about the cast of his 2012 championship. Ball-hawks were led by long-stick middie Scott Ratliff and short-stick defensive middie Josh Hawkins. Justin Ward choreographed an attack which featured two fifty-goal players, namely, Eric Lusby and Mike Sawyer. Sean O'Sullivan had transferred in from Army. Chris Lane transferred from UNC. They were stout middies, and Jack Runkle was superb in the goal. Joe Fletcher began his three-year run as an All-American defenseman with countless take-aways. Reid Acton was another very strong defenseman who also wreaked havoc on the highly rated Maryland attack. And Dave Butts was another stellar member of the Hounds deep midfield group, which ran and ran. During the semi-final and the final, Loyola allowed a total of eight goals. That has never happened before or since in the NCAA tournament.

A remarkable factor about this historic run to the championship lies in the fact that the Hounds played a Bill Tierney-led team, Denver, three times this season. Tierney is the Nick Saban of lacrosse, having won six titles with Princeton before going west to Colorado. Loyola at this time was a member of the ECAC and played Denver in the regular season, then in the conference tournament. Having won both of these games, they faced the Pioneers again in the quarterfinals at the Naval Academy. It took a left-handed burner from Brian Schultz in overtime to secure the third win against Denver and send the Hounds to the final four.

Coach Toomey is an institution now at Evergreen. He is fast approaching the win total of Coach Cottle. His philosophy is to make the players better persons, students, and players, in that order. Make all practices meaningful and learning experiences, justifying hard practices, featuring lots of running, ala USNA. Finally, along with absorbing the Jesuit culture, establish and maintain a culture of winning.

L

The magical, mystery tour of seven years was operable three times. For Jay Connor, it was a seven-year run to the NCAA D-II title game in 1981. For Dave Cottle, it was a seven-year climb to the NCAA D-I title game in 1990. For Charley Toomey, it was a seven-year quest to the NCAA D-I title game in 2012. Following the 2012 title, another seven-year period for Charley was tolled. That would make the year of 2019 a time for another title game. It was not to be. But the seasons after the title win branded the Hounds as an elite team. All opponents now perceived the Hounds as a team that was well-coached, superbly conditioned, and formidable. There would never again be a "massacre" series. The Hounds would dominate the Patriot League with all its stellar schools. They would produce more All Americans. During this time span they would produce, in all probability, its finest goalie, defenseman, attackman, and long-stick midfielder in its history.

L

Matt Stover was an All-Pro kicker for many seasons with the Baltimore Ravens of the NFL. He was a staunch Christian. Although not a Catholic, he told me that he would have sent his son, Jacob, to Loyola, even if Jacob had not been recruited by Charley. Matt appreciates the value and character-building of the Jesuit education. My son, Brendan, attended a youth soccer camp of Matt's many years ago. Brendan still has a signed Bible that Matt gave to all the young attendees. I pray Brendan might read it someday. Jake was a first-team All-Metro out of McDonogh (where my daughter Eileen was a star cheerleader), and consequently had numerous offers. Fortunately, he chose Loyola. He became the first of a long line of great Hound goalies to receive first-team D-I All-American honors. Several previous goalies had garnered second and third-team honors, including coach Toomey. And there were some honorable mentions over the years. Actually, during the war years of World War II, when there was a dearth of teams (fifteen), a Hound did make first-team All American in the goal. The year was 1943, and his name was Gerry Courtney. The following year the Hounds shut down the team. Gerry's selection has a Roger Maris asterisk.

Marty "Skip" Barry and Bill Flattery were honorable mention goal keepers of the fifties. Harry Bregel was honorable mention in the sixties. Steve McCloskey was first-team in 1981, but that was for D-II In 1988, Tom McClelland was second team. Then coach Toomey was honorable mention in '89 and third-team in '90. Tim McGeeney had a great run in his sophomore, junior, and senior years in the goal from '93 through '95. He was honorable mention, third-team, and second-team. He was a great goalie. In 1999 Jim Brown was third-team, and Jack Runkle was second team in 2014. Every year the competition gets stiffer because of the strength of the D-I teams. Jake Stover started as a freshman in 2016. That year Pat Spencer was also a freshman, and they carried the team into the Final Four at Lincoln Financial Field in Philadelphia. Forty thousand fans sat in sweltering heat as Loyola had difficulty overcoming an early 9–1 deficit. They were up against a team that was on a mission. North Carolina won 18–13 and then prevailed in overtime against Maryland two days later for the championship.

That marked the last time the Hounds made it to the final four. But Pat Spencer and Jake Stover will be sorely missed. Spencer won the Tewaaraton award as the country's finest player. It was well deserved. He was Lamar Jackson with a stick. He had many remarkable games over his four years. He was an All American all four years, and first team for each of his last three years. He surpassed Gary Hanley as the all-time point leader for the Hounds. In his final tournament appearance in 2019, he seemed to be either feeding or scoring every goal in the 21–14 loss to Penn State. He was a joy to watch.

Pat gives due credit. "Coach Toomey gave me the green light from day one to play my game and lead the offense." Charley confides: "We knew we were getting a talented kid. But we didn't have any idea of the beast that was going to step on the field for us as a freshman." Pat adds, "I've had incredible teammates, and the coaching staff has always been incredible." Pat is now off to Northwestern in Chicago for grad school, where he will bring his super talents to the basketball court.

Needless to say, Pat would be a unanimous pick as player of the decade from 2010-2019. He is a unanimous choice as the player of all-time for Loyola. We didn't pick a player of the first decade of the century because of the dark years. But Shane Koppens and Andy Spack were a strong twosome in the middle of the decade. At the end of the decade there was the dynamic duo of Mike Sawyer and Eric Lusby. They all get a handshake in deference to a trophy. Lusby and Sawyer are already immortalized for the 2012 title.

L

Chris Gunkle has seen a lot over his years as a player and then as a game announcer. Chris was a midfielder on the 1990 team, his senior year. He played with us on the Thunder. He eventually moved to North Carolina for business reasons. He returned after about ten years and began a new affinity for the Hounds. When Sean Smith retired as an announcer in 2002, Chris was asked to step in. He's bee announcing ever since. He relates that when Pat Spencer was a sophomore at Boys Latin, colleges were recruiting players in the ninth grade. Now the NCAA has passed a rule that forbids contact until September of the junior years in high school. Pat was injured during his sophomore year and not noticed very much. And he was only on the JV team. When he became a star in his third year, most colleges had stocked their barns with a full quota of players, most of whom were recruited out of the ninth or tenth grade. Charley had room for Pat and grabbed him. As Gary Hanley was my best recruit, Pat was Charley's.

L

On the 2012 championship team, Joe Fletcher was a standout sophomore defenseman. In his junior and senior years, he was first-team All American. In his senior year he captured the William C. Schmeisser Award for the nation's best defenseman. He was the Patriot League's defenseman of the year. In the classroom, he was the Patriot League student-athlete of the year. He was the only player still in college to be picked on Team USA in 2014. In 2015, he was honored as the defender of the year for Major League Lacrosse.

Another sophomore on that 2012 team was Justin Ward. In 2012 he was flanked by Mike Sawyer and Eric Lusby, both seniors. Two years later, Justin was the show as he set a Patriot League record for assists with fifty-three. He was also the league's offensive player of the year. And he was a second-team All American.

During this seven-year period, several players stood out. Brian Sherlock was an honorable mention, second and third-team All American as a middie with a hard shot. Nikko Pontrello played attack with Ward in 2014 and earned an honorable mention nod. Unfortunately, that team lost in the first round of the NCAAs to an Albany team that was a sleeper with the Thompson brothers, who were co-Tewaaraton winners. All of Charley's teams during this seven- year span were in the NCAAs except the 2015 team. That was a team that lost six games by one goal and became Charley's second team with a losing record. This time frame produced some excellent defensemen in addition to Joe Fletcher. There was Reed Acton, Pat Frazier, and Foster Huggins, among others. Pat Laconi was a stellar short-stick defensive middie. This was the role of Josh Hawkins, who played on the championship rope unit with Scott Ratliff. Josh was recruited out of the Deerfield Academy in Massachusetts.

Scott was one of those obscure recruits that Charley uncovered. He was from Atlanta and played on the Westminster High School team coached by John Holthaus, another ex-Thunder player. John had alerted Charley of Scott, but Charley had someone else in mind as a LSM. Among all colleges, only the Naval Academy had recruited Scott. When the player Charley wanted went elsewhere, he called John Holthaus to see if Scott was still available. John said Scott was ready to report to Navy for plebe summer induction. Charley called Scott and determined that he would love to come to Loyola but he was committed to Navy and feared he couldn't extricate himself from the appointment. As a precaution, Charley also called Scott's parents, who at the time were vacationing in Hawaii. They gave their okay to Loyola. Charley, using his Navy contacts, called Ritchie Meade, the Navy coach. He was able to liberate Scott from the Navy commitment. Scott became a two-time All American. He may be the greatest LSM ever to wear the Hound green. He went on to be a star in the MLL.

𝕃

Chris Gunkle reminded me of Vinny Pfieffer's athleticism. Vinny had transferred to Loyola in 1984 from U of B, which had foreclosed all its sports teams, including lacrosse. He was a terrific goalie, but only had one year of eligibility remaining upon his transfer. After graduating from Loyola, he joined the long list of heralded volunteer assistants whom Dave Cottle managed to commandeer. Vinny, like myself, loved to take the team on long runs. The boys protested just as my troops protested to me. My trick was to stay in the back of the slow-moving stampede of runners. Then I would systematically pass the herd while shouting commentary like "get the lead out!" Vinny's ploy was to get far ahead, then climb a tree. From his clandestine perch on a strong branch, he would stealthily shout down his derisive commentary as the players passed below. His verbal assaults of players dogging it often were heard without the players knowing from where the voice came. What fun!

Gunks, like Matt Dwan, confirms the terror Cottle could impose on the players, as well as revealing a softer side. Bill Dirrigl, a Cottle paid assistant, told the players in the locker room on an otherwise nice, sunny day, that they should be prepared for a tough practice, that something has gotten Coach ticked off and he is in a lousy mood. The boys suited up for practice and gingerly drifted onto the Evergreen field waiting for a coach explosion. Cottle ambled out onto the field dragging a huge duffle bag. Anticipation was wearing them down. Suddenly, Dave opens the bag and dumps out the contents. It was bats, bases, gloves, and softballs. Dave said "We need to relax for a change. Let's choose up sides and have a softball game." And so they did, and peace returned to the Hound ten.

Chris says one of the more memorable games that he broadcast was the 2012 game at Ridley versus Hopkins. Loyola was playing its last game of the year and was undefeated. A win would ensure a high seed in the NCAAs. Hopkins was also expecting a high seed, as they had lost but one game. Ridley was rocking with over six thousand fans. The stands were packed like sardines in a tin. Fans were standing on the grassy hill on the north side of the field behind the fence. This area was accessible because of a reunion tent party in the pavilion area above the grassy hill. The crowd was augmented by the large traveling Jay supporters, including students, alums, and the perpetual group-think worshipers. It was a battle of the two premier local teams. Chris said that he was constantly getting texts and emails during the game complaining that his voice and Dave's could not be heard because of the constant noise din of the crowd. The game was also being streamed out across the country and set a record for market subscribers. It caused the need for rewiring the bands to handle the growing TV audiences. Loyola trailed by five goals late in the game but mounted a furious rally to tie and send the game into overtime. This would be the Hounds lone loss in their championship run.

L

Chris relates that Coach Cottle was maniacal about beating Towson. He felt that Loyola was a better school with better academics and a higher quality of student and that they should never be bested by Towson or

even UMBC, another local school he deemed inferior to Loyola. In Chris'
freshman year, the Hounds lost to Towson. It so infuriated Dave that he
arranged a scrimmage the following morning. He assembled an all-star
cast of players like John Tucker, Pat Lamon, Dave Pietramala, Vinny
Pfieffer, and others and let them suit up against the Hounds. Chris said
it was a torturous two hours but "we learned a lot." They didn't lose
again to Towson during Gunk's four years. During these years, Hopkins
was not on the schedule, as the "massacre" had not as yet been resumed.

Gunks points out that Dave didn't have the resources that are
available today. Kroney characterizes those years as teams "not fully
funded." Dave looked on the Evergreen field as a glorified "damn
parking lot" and an albatross to the program. The synthetic-turf field
had become quite worn and hard. But he was driven to succeed despite shortcomings in what he could offer.

Another rival acquired during the Hopkins freeze out was Georgetown. Dave reflected the attitude of the administration. Georgetown
was a rival Jesuit school which was envisioned as superior to Loyola.
It graduated congressman and presidents, DC lawyers and lobbyists.
Loyola graduated professionals who stayed in Baltimore, a backwater,
blue-collar town. Furthermore, Georgetown was a national basketball
power with an NCAA title. Dave did his part to atone for the secondary image of Loyola's Jesuit profile by beating Georgetown regularly.
Charley continued this trend by annually besting the Hoyas of Washington, DC.

L

When the 1990 season began, the first game was at Rutgers in Piscataway, New Jersey. As the bus entered the campus, Dave started complaining that the field was changed from the carpeted stadium to

another field with natural grass. Dave said that was breaking a contract and that the Hounds should use that as motivation to beat the cheaters. He then had the bus drive to the stadium and had everyone get out and walk onto the field. He pointed out that this was where the championship game would be played. "Let's be here at season's end." The Hounds met that expectation and came full circle. They beat Rutgers that day and beat them again in the quarterfinals to go to the finals at this stadium.

L

There was a particularly agonizing loss at Evergreen to Duke in Dirrigl's last season. After the game, several high college officials, including AD Joe Boylan, were lingering on the field, lamenting how the program had regressed. Something must be done! Before season's end the Hounds would also lose to Georgetown, Towson, UMBC, and Hopkins, in route to a 5–8 year. Coach Dirrigl was dismissed. Not long after this beheading, Father Hap Ridley died in his sleep at his Millbrook Road residence. The Ridley Stadium, not yet named, was still on the drawing board. The new president, Brian Linane, S.J., jumped in with both feet. He rallied the board. He sent advocates to City Hall to secure the votes to confirm the purchase from the city. He sent envoys to neighborhood meetings to assuage fears that the stadium complex would be disruptive to the environment and to the peace of the community. The earth began to move, and the cement was soon being poured into the side of the hill, which used to be a city dump. The stadium rose majestically, and Loyola became totally legitimate as a D-I lacrosse force to be reckoned with. Fr. Linane told the board, most unselfishly, that the complex should be named after Fr. Harold "Hap" Ridley. And so it was.

L

Many tales from the days at the old Evergreen field live on. During the Cottle era, Skip Evans was the equipment manager. He succeeded Bobby Harmon and Wilson Bean. Skip's brother, Don, was a standout goalie for City and BU. Skip did not really have a lacrosse background. We were always suspect of Skip's formal education or lack thereof. But, like Bean and Bobby, he was a loveable guy. He in turn loved lacrosse and the team. He was always there behind the bench at games at Evergreen. His antics during the game were classic and probably would not be tolerated now. Skip would run up and down the sidelines screaming encouragement to the Hounds. He would also scream derogatory remarks at the opponent. Sometimes opposing coaches would complain. Cottle would ignore them or tell them he didn't know the guy but he heard he had escaped from the Shepherd Pratt asylum and could be dangerous. He best be ignored.

Dennis Townsend, of abundant ignominy for outbidding Ed Hale and me in buying the Thunder, was one of the myriad of assistants who wandered onto Cottle's practices. But Dennis was actually a great defenseman from Hopkins and a genuinely good coach. But his arrival at practices always raised eyebrows. He was a wealthy developer. He would arrive in an exotic car wearing Brooks Brother suits and ties. He also would bring his cell phone to discuss business while the players were going through their drills. In those pre iPhone days, the cell phones were as big as a radio on steroids. And they weighed perhaps thirty pounds. Seriously. The players thought it might be an explosive device that he was going to detonate as a spy from Hopkins. But Dennis turned out to be a good guy and a great help in the 1990 title run.

During a spring break sometime in the mid-nineties, Loyola had agreed to let W & L practice on the Evergreen field. W & L was in town to play another D-III school at a neutral site the following day. Dave was told by the AD Joe Boylan to vacate the field early. As the bus pulled up and the preppy kids from W & L disembarked, Dave told his players to remain and take a good look at the profile of kids from an elite southern school. Then he ordered the Hounds to begin a spirited scrimmage until the Generals arrived on the field. Dave didn't like W & L because it was the antithesis of his background. But he wanted the Generals to see his troops and know that we were indeed better than them. At least in lacrosse! I hearken to the game of yesteryear, on this very field, when I earned my nickname of Diamond playing against the Washington and Lee Generals.

L

One must take as hard evidence the quality of Loyola lacrosse coaches over the past few decades. Many coaches and players have fallen from the Loyola tree and gone on to be successful coaches elsewhere. Bobby Benson has been the offensive coordinator for Hopkins for several years. He began as an assistant for Charley. Assistants Ryan Moran and Dan Chemoti are the head coaches at UMBC and Richmond, respectively. Dave Allen is still on the staff at Gilman. John Tucker has had stints at several MIAA schools and is now at Curley. Don Zimmerman went on to be the head coach at UMBC for many years. Dave Pietramala got his start helping Cottle. Paul Canabene has had great success at Stevenson as head coach. Ditto Kevin Anderson at Notre Dame and Chris Colbeck at Villanova, who are long- time assistants. And there are others.

Often Charley will end up facing a coach who began on his staff. It worked the other way in 1993 when he was the head coach at

NAPS. Loyola was to play Navy in a tournament game, and Ritchie Meade, the Navy coach, asked Charley for some info on the Hounds. As Charley was a Navy employee, he complied. He later received a call from a familiar voice that said, "You are Benedict Arnold." It was Dave Cottle. To this day Charley doesn't know whether Dave was kidding or acting out of his intense nature. The answer will not be found in these pages. You will only find a story of rags to riches with smiles along the way. Perhaps you will perceive the hand of God orchestrating a lacrosse odyssey at Loyola University Maryland.

L

Some may be disappointed that these pages are not filled with enough names. And that the book lacks statistics, pictures, and game summaries. That was not my intent. I just wanted to tell a story of how Loyola, coming from nowhere, climbed to an elite status in a wonderful game. It became more personal than I originally intended. But lacrosse has been important to me. I was never happier than when I was on the field with the Hounds. Even my days coaching my four kids were not quite as pleasurable as my days with the Hounds. Coaching my kids brought stress from the other parents as well as from my kids themselves. When we won, mealtime was happy. When we lost, there were glum faces at the table. When I think back on my years of coaching Hounds, I see only smiling young faces.

I had often mused, as a young lawyer, that if someone could get the attention of the administration at Loyola, a very successful lacrosse team could be placed on the field. And it would mean something in this lacrosse mecca of Baltimore. By happenstance, I was given this opportunity. I became a change agent. I want no plaudits. If not me, someone ese would have come along and perhaps have had a providential conversation with a Loyola president. Thank you again, Fr. Joe. Keep throwing down those blessings on the Greyhounds lacrosse team.

My years with the Thunder were also very satisfying years. Many of the players quoted in this modest project were members of my Thunder teams. Others quoted played on rival MILL teams but were Hound alums. I thank them all for their memories and time. AMDG.

"Let us put on faith and love for a breastplate and the hope of salvation for a helmet."

—1 Thessalonians 5:8

BIBLIOGRAPHY

Calder, Jim and Fletcher, Ron. *Lacrosse: The American Game.* Toronto, Ontario, Canada: Canadian Cataloging Publications, 2011.

Carpenter, Robert. *Lacrosse: North America's Game.* Towson, Maryland: Carpenter Publishing Co., 2005.

Fisher, Donald M. *Lacrosse: A History of the Game.* Baltimore, Maryland: The Johns Hopkins University Press, 2002.

Flynn, Tom. *Men's Lacrosse in Maryland.* Charleston, South Carolina: The History Press, 2016.

McDonough, Peter. *Men Astutely Trained: History of the Jesuits in the American Century.* New York, NY. : Macmillan, Inc., 1992.

Russell, Jr., G. Darrell. *Hotbed for Hybrids: Soccer and Lacrosse in Baltimore.* Glen Burnie, Maryland: French Bray Printing Company, 1978.

Scott, Bob. *Lacrosse: Fundamentals and Tradition.* Baltimore, Maryland: Johns Hopkins University Press, 1976.

Weyand, Alexander M. and Roberts, Milton R. *The Lacrosse Story.* Baltimore, Maryland: Pridemark Press, Inc., 1964.

Yeager, John M. *Our Game: The Character and Culture of Lacrosse.* Port Chester, New York: Duse Publishing Co., 2006.